Minister

as Jesus Ministered

BOOK 4 EXPERIENCE THE LIFE

Minister
as Jesus Ministered

Transformed Service

BILL HULL & PAUL MASCARELLA

NAVPRESS
Discipleship Inside Out™

NAVPRESS
Discipleship Inside Out™

NavPress is the publishing ministry of The Navigators, an international Christian organization and leader in personal spiritual development. NavPress is committed to helping people grow spiritually and enjoy lives of meaning and hope through personal and group resources that are biblically rooted, culturally relevant, and highly practical.

For a free catalog go to www.NavPress.com
or call 1.800.366.7788 in the United States or 1.800.839.4769 in Canada.

ISBN-13: 978-1-61521-543-0

Cover design by Arvid Wallen
Cover image by Shutterstock

Printed in the United States of America

1 2 3 4 5 6 7 8 / 14 13 12 11 10

CONTENTS

INTRODUCTION

To *experience the life* is to commit to a way or pattern of life. Its basis is humility and it is a life of self-denial and submission to others. The life that Jesus lived and prescribed for us is different from the one being offered by many churches. His servant leadership was radically distinct from what is extolled by secular society and even too bold for what is modeled in the Christian community. This life is essentially the *faith of following*, of taking up one's cross daily and following Him. It is fundamentally about giving up the right to run your own life. It is living the life that Jesus lived, the life to which He has called every disciple.

To put it another way, we can only experience the life Jesus has called us to by committing to training that will enable us to believe as Jesus believed, live as Jesus lived, love as Jesus loved, minister as Jesus ministered, and lead as Jesus led.

It is only by taking Jesus' discipling yoke upon ourselves that can experience the life that Jesus lived. Only then will we discover its light burden and enjoy His promised "rest for [our] souls" (Matthew 11:29-30).

ABOUT THIS BOOK

This book is the fourth in the five-book EXPERIENCE THE LIFE series. It continues the thirty-week course, built upon the ideas introduced and developed in Bill Hull's book *Choose the Life,* which begins with the series' first book, *Believe as Jesus Believed.*

Its Purpose

EXPERIENCE THE LIFE exists to assist the motivated disciple in entering into a more profound way of thinking and living. That way is the pattern of life Jesus modeled and then called every interested person to follow. Simply put, it is the living out of Jesus' life by: believing as Jesus believed, living as Jesus lived, loving as Jesus loved, ministering as Jesus ministered, and leading as Jesus led. This *Life* is a life grounded in humility—characterized by submission, obedience, suffering, and the joys of exaltation. It is the life that transforms its adherents and penetrates the strongest resistance. It then calls upon each person to rethink what it means to be a follower of Jesus.

This book is the fourth in the five-book EXPERIENCE THE LIFE series. It is designed to lead disciples in a thirty-week course, built upon the ideas introduced and developed in Bill Hull's book *Choose the Life.* It provides a daily format that directs a disciple's thinking toward the application of these truths, thereby producing in him a faith hospitable to healthy spiritual transformation—*a faith that embraces discipleship.*

Its Participants

Virtually all significant change can, should be, and eventually is tested in relationship to others. To say that one is more loving without it being verified in relation to others is hollow. Not only do others need to be involved to test one's progress, they are needed to encourage and help someone else in the journey of transformation. Therefore, going on the journey with others is absolutely necessary.

The five books are designed to lead each disciple in a personal journey of spiritual formation by participation within a community of disciples, who have likewise decided to *experience the life*.

The community is composed of (optimally) from two to eight disciples being led in this thirty-week course to *experience the life*.

Participants in the community agree to make time and perform the daily assignments as directed in each book. They have agreed to pray daily for the other members of their community and to keep whatever is shared at their community meeting in confidence. They will attend and fully participate in each weekly community meeting.

Its Process

We recognize that all change, all spiritual transformation, is the result of a process. Events may instigate change in people; they may provide the motive, the occasion, and the venue for change to begin, but the changes that result in healthy spiritual transformation are the product of a process.

We can glean a description of the transformational process from the apostle Paul's command in Romans 12:2:

Do not conform any longer to the pattern of this world, but be transformed by the renewing of your mind. Then you will be able to test and approve what God's will is—his good, pleasing and perfect will.

This process of transformation asserts that the believer must no longer conform to what is false, the "pattern of this world" (its ideas and values, and the behaviors which express them). Also, he must be transformed, which means his pattern must be changed, conformed to another pattern (the truth), which is not "of this world." This is done by the process of "the renewing of your mind." What does it mean to renew something? To what is Paul referring when he says that the mind must undergo this renewal?

To renew something means to act upon something in ways that will cause it to be as it was when it was new. The principle idea is one of restoring something that is currently malfunctioning and breaking down to its fully functioning state, its original pristine state, the state it was in prior to it sustaining any damage. We must avoid the modern notion that renewing something means simply replacing the old thing with an entirely new thing. Paul, and the people to whom he wrote these words, would simply not understand *renew* to mean anything like what we moderns mean when we use the word *replace*. They would understand that renewing the wheels on one's cart meant repairing them to their fully functioning state. And so, what Paul means by "being transformed by the *renewing* of your mind" (emphasis ours) is that the mind must undergo changes, repairs that will restore it to its original condition, the fully functioning state it enjoyed when it was first created. As these repairs proceed in the restoration/renewal process and a detrimental modification to the original design is discovered, that modification must be removed. It must be removed so that it will not interfere with its operating as it was originally designed. Further, to properly renew anything, we must understand its original design. The best way to renew something is with the direction and assistance of the original builder. A builder in Paul's day was not only the builder but also the designer and architect. With the expertise and help available through the builder, full renewal is best accomplished.

If you are renewing a house, that house's builder would best know how to go about it. If you are renewing an automobile, that automobile's builder would best know how to go about it. In our case, we are renewing the mind. It stands to reason, then, that its renewal would best be accomplished in partnership with its Architect/Builder — God.

We know that it is the mind that is to be renewed, and that we should partner with God to accomplish its renewal, but what is it about the mind that is being renewed? Is it broken, in need of new parts?

When Paul says that it is the mind which is being renewed when spiritual transformation is taking place, he means much more than what most of us think of when we use the word *mind*. Most of us think of the mind as some sort of calculator in our head, so it's understandable that our idea of renewing it would start with the idea of replacing its broken parts. But for Paul, the mind is much more than a calculator in our head, and to renew it means more than simply swapping out a sticky key, or a cracked screen, or replacing the batteries that have run low.

The Greek word that Paul uses and is translated as the English word mind is νους. Here it means the inner direction of one's thoughts and will and the orientation of one's moral consciousness. When Paul refers to our mind's renewal, he is saying that the current direction of our thoughts and will must be changed. The way our mind currently directs our thoughts and will no longer leads to where the mind was originally designed to take our thoughts and will. Our mind no longer leads our thinking to know the will of God, to know what is good, pleasing, and perfect, and no longer directs our will to accomplish God's will, to do what is good, pleasing, and perfect. This is in large part what is meant by being lost. If our minds are not renewed, then we cannot live a life directed toward doing what is pleasing to God. We need to undergo the restoration process that will return our minds to operating as they were originally designed, allowing our minds to direct our thinking and will toward God. The good news is that the original Builder/Architect—God—prescribed the renewing of the mind as the sure remedy to restoring us to spiritual health, and He intends to partner with us in this restoration process.

For spiritual transformation to occur there must be a partnership between the Holy Spirit and the person who is to undergo transformation. It is good news that the Holy Spirit is involved in the process of our restoration because, unlike other things that undergo restoration, like houses, tables, and chairs, we are not just passive things. We are more. We are *beings*, *human* beings, *made* in the image of God. Being made in the image of God includes much more than I will (or even can) mention, but for our purposes it includes having thoughts, ideas, passions, desires, and a will of our own. Because these abilities in their current condition (i.e. before renewal) no longer lead us toward God's will, we do not have the ability to direct our own transformation. We need someone who is not "conformed to the pattern of this world," one who is completely conformed to the will of God, to direct the renewal. And because we are in this prerenewal condition, we need someone to initiate, to enable us, and encourage us to continue the process, someone who is not subject to the same problems our condition allows. Who is better to direct than God? Who is better to enable and encourage than God? There is none better suited to the task than the Holy Spirit. That we are partnering with Him is good news indeed!

With the initiating, enabling, and direction of the Holy Spirit, the process of renewal can begin. It is a two-stage process: the *appropriation of the truth* and the *application of truth-directed behavior.* The first stage, the *appropriation of the truth*, takes place when:

1. We have the desire to pursue the Truth to be changed;
2. We then act upon that desire, choosing to pursue the Truth by setting our will.

The second stage, the *application of truth-directed behavior*, takes place when:

1. We begin practicing behaviors, which we'll describe as spiritual disciplines, designed to halt our conformity to "the pattern of this world";
2. We engage in transformational activities, which are designed to reorient our mind and direct it toward God's will;
3. We continue to practice transformational activities to introduce and establish new patterns of thinking and behavior which conform our mind to the mind of Christ.

The same components in the process for renewing the mind that we gleaned from the apostle Paul can also be seen in Jesus' call to anyone who would follow Him.

Jesus commanded all who would follow Him (all disciples) to:

> Come to me, all you who are weary and burdened, and I will
> give you rest. Take my yoke upon you and learn from me, for I
> am gentle and humble in heart, and you will find rest for your
> souls. (Matthew 11:28-29)

Jesus begins with a promise, "Come . . . and I will give you rest." He
kindles a desire to follow Him. This is the first step in *the appropriation
of truth*, the *desire* to pursue the truth. We *desire* change. Next is Jesus'
command to take His yoke. This is the second step in the *appropriation
of truth*, *choosing* to pursue the truth. We set our *will* to change. At this
step, we can choose to pursue our desire for the truth and change or
ignore it. If we choose to delay placing it upon our shoulders it is at the
cost of rest to our souls. The choice precedes the action. Next, we read
that we are to take His yoke.

To take His yoke is the first step of the second stage in the process
of renewing the mind, the *application of truth-directed behavior*. At this
step, as we saw before with Paul, we discontinue with our current ways,
which conform us to the pattern of this world. We intentionally begin
to dislodge the destructive patterns that have grown in us as a precursor
to the second step, the taking-upon of a new way, God's way, His yoke.

The second step, the taking-upon of Jesus' yoke, is the part of the
process of renewing the mind where the vacancy left from dislodging
our old ways, "the pattern of this world," is being filled up with the new
life-giving patterns by which we are to conform our lives. It is this yoke,
God's new way of living the life that Jesus lived, that is to be taken upon
us. Just as the yoke for an ox is placed upon its body, allowing the power
of the ox to perform its master's work (work the ox would otherwise
not be able to accomplish), so also Jesus' yoke must be placed upon our
body to allow it to perform our Master's work, the renewing of our mind
(work we would otherwise not be able to accomplish).

Finally, we see the third, and last step, in the *application of truth-
directed behavior*. This is the final step in the process of renewal, but it
is also the beginning step in the ongoing process of our spiritual transformation. It finally brings us all the way to our taking Jesus' yoke upon

us. It also begins the continuing journey of knowing and doing God's good, pleasing, and perfect will. While the second step trains the mind by establishing patterns, the third step lives out the new character that is replacing the old. This continuing journey begins once we take His yoke upon us. For then we begin to "learn from me [Jesus]" and thereby experience rest for our soul. This rest, this peacefulness that comes from learning from Jesus, is what it is to live with a renewed mind. It is experiencing the Spirit-initiated, encouraged, enabled, and empowered life Jesus enjoyed with the peace that comes only by having the "mind of Christ" and by accomplishing His good, pleasing, and perfect will.

EXPERIENCE THE LIFE provides the disciple a structured process whereby he can engage in the process of spiritual renewal. It provides a daily regimen for practicing specific disciplines designed to displace those old destructive ideas and behaviors (the patterns of the world) and replacing them with new, constructive, life-giving ideas and behaviors (the mind of Christ).

EXPERIENCE THE LIFE requires commitment to consistently practice the disciplines and to reserve the time required for transformation.

Most studies on change agree that displacing a current habit or idea and establishing a new one requires a minimum of about three months. Also, learning studies demonstrate the necessity of consistent application of the thing being learned to ensure its permanent retention.

According to a leading learning researcher, people remember:

- 10% of what they read
- 20% of what they hear
- 30% of what they see
- 50% of what they see and hear
- 70% of what they say
- 95% of what they teach someone else[1]

1. William Glassner, *Control Therapy in the Classroom* (New York: Harper and Row, 1986); *Reality Therapy: A New Approach to Psychiatry* (New York: Harper and Row, 1965).

Simply put, we learn best not by passively hearing and seeing, but by actively "doing" the thing which we are learning.

The most relevant question a teacher can ask is, "Are my students learning?" For our purposes, the relevant question must be, "Am I engaged in a process that will result in my being changed from what I am into what I am to be? Am I being transformed into the image of Christ?"

Each book in this series provides a solid opportunity for significant transformation through the use of several common tools or disciplines including:

- Reading Scripture together
- Reading a common philosophy of the Christian experience
- Journaling insights, questions, and prayers
- Discussion over material that has already been studied, prayed over, and reflected upon
- Accountability for the purpose of helping each other keep their commitments to God
- Encouragement to help each other overcome areas of defeat and break free of bondage
- Mutual commitment to apply what God has impressed on each member
- Mutual commitment to impact those with whom they have contact

Its Pattern

This course leads the believer to *experience the life* Jesus lived, utilizing a daily regimen to practice the various spiritual disciplines. The course is thirty weeks long over five books.

The five books, each six weeks in length, instruct and challenge the disciple to conform his life to:

1. Believe as Jesus believed,
2. Live as Jesus lived,
3. Love as Jesus loved,

4. Minister as Jesus ministered, and

5. Lead as Jesus led.

Each six-week book leads disciples through a course of daily teachings and exercises in an examination of how Jesus lived out His faith.

In daily session five, the disciple begins with a prayer focused on the issues to be presented in the daily reading. The daily reading gives a core thought that will be explored in the day's exercises. Questions are designed to help the disciple's understanding of the core thoughts and key ideas. Disciples are then directed to reflect on the application of these core thoughts and key ideas to their own spiritual growth. Journaling space is provided for answering questions and recording thoughts, questions, applications, and insights stemming from their reflection.

Once weekly (the sixth session), the disciple meets with others who comprise their community. At the community meeting they pray together, discuss the core thoughts and key ideas introduced in the week's readings, and share from their own experience of practicing the week's spiritual discipline. They view and discuss the video introduction for the following week's study and pray and encourage one another in their journey of spiritual transformation.

Although the books were designed primarily for use by groups consisting of two to six members, the material and the format can easily be used to effectively lead larger groups in a discussion-based exploration of spiritual transformation.

Lastly, we recommend that the leaders of the weekly discussion groups proceed through each book together as a community group prior to leading their own group. The insights that they will acquire from their own journey through EXPERIENCE THE LIFE will be invaluable to them and the larger group they will lead.

When leading a larger group through EXPERIENCE THE LIFE, keep in mind that most of the spiritual traction for transformation is due to the interaction that the Lord has with each individual through the other individuals in a community of believers. To preserve this traction, the leader must provide a venue and time for this interaction. For this reason, we suggest that some time during the weekly session, the leader divide the large group into smaller groups mimicking the two- to six-member community group for the purpose of more intimately discussing the issues presented in the week's session. It is reported after experiencing successive weeks with the same members of this smaller discussion group individuals previously not participants in a small-group program have desired to continue in such a program.

While we believe that the most effective and efficient means of leading individuals to healthy spiritual transformation is in the context of a smaller community group, we do acknowledge that the larger group setting may be the only means currently available to a church's leadership. Though the *form* of instruction is important, the *function* is what must be preserved: *Verum supremus vultus* (truth above form).

Its Product

Each session is designed to challenge the disciple to examine the progress of his own transformation, to train him with the desire to both know God's will and do it. This course values the spiritual traction the disciple can get by facing this challenge in a high-trust community. Christ was a Man for others. Disciples then are to be people for others. It is only in losing ourselves in the mission of loving others that we live in balance and experience the joy that Christ has promised. And therein lie many of the rewards a disciple may enjoy as he lives and loves as Jesus. This is the life that cultivates Christlikeness and whose product is a transformed disciple—the only life of faith worthy of justifying our calling upon others to EXPERIENCE THE LIFE.

WEEK ONE

Call to Ministry

DAY ONE

Prayer

Dear Lord, I don't mind doing nice things for people. I like to help out people when they're in a jam. What I don't like is to be gushed all over about something that I have done. Please help me to stop being so caught up in what others might be thinking about me. Help me to become less self-concerned. Amen.

Core Thought

> The call to ministry is a command to display profoundly heroic character.

The call to ministry is Jesus' command to His disciples that they become one another's servants. To minister means to serve, and serving requires two things, submission and obedience. For service to take place there must be an attitude of willingness present within us that will allow us to submit to someone else's program and allow us to act in obedience to someone else's plan. Jesus demonstrated His attitude toward His own mission when He said, "For even the Son of Man did not come to be served, but to serve, and to give his life as a ransom for many" (Mark 10:45). This attitude has largely eluded contemporary leaders because you can't give yourself as a sacrifice and at the same time manage your image.

This willingness to sacrifice oneself for the sake of others and for a purpose greater than one's own benefit is the essential quality we honor in those we call heroes. How common is this quality? Let's admit that it's rare enough that when someone exhibits this quality, we call it heroic. We bestow medals on police officers, soldiers, firefighters, and others who risk life and limb to pull people out of a burning home or pluck a drowning child from a lake.

I don't want to diminish acts of heroism. However, I'm talking about something greater than one heroic moment in someone's life. I think Jesus modeled and taught a more profound heroism—a heroism of character and purpose that produces a steady stream of sacrificial actions.

Can you imagine a life so lost in benefiting others that your personal needs and wants don't play a big role in your thoughts? Love, after all, means action directed toward the benefiting of others. And Jesus' calling of us to ministry to serve others is simply a continuance of His original commands to love our neighbors and to love one another as He has loved us. For us to obey these commands will require our having the same profoundly self-sacrificing heroism of character that Jesus' willingness displayed.

Today's Exercises
Core Scripture: 2 Corinthians 2 and 3
Read aloud 2 Corinthians 2:14-17; 3:4-6,17-18.
Recite this week's memory verse aloud five times.

> He has made us competent as ministers of a new covenant—
> not of the letter but of the Spirit; for the letter kills, but the
> Spirit gives life. (2 Corinthians 3:6)

Meditate on today's passage.

Request to Be in His Presence
"Dear Lord, bring me into the context of Your world."

1. ***Read it***—Remember: We read now only what is there, to hear once again, only what was spoken then. Read 1 Peter 1:1 at least twice, out loud.

2. ***Think it***—select a portion, a phrase within the reading, and mull it over in your mind, thinking about the context and setting, reimagining the event, putting yourself into the situation. As you meditate, use all five senses to re-create the context and the setting by building the images that are supplied within the passages.

3. ***Pray it***—ask God to give you understanding into how the truths He has spoken in these Scriptures apply to you now. Ask, "What is it about me that I need to deal with? What is it about me that must change?"

   Respond to God by accepting and admitting whatever responsibility is implied by what He has shown. Write what it is that God has shown you, and what you must admit responsibility for having done (or not done).

4. ***Live it***—ask God to reveal to you what He wants you to do about what you have admitted.

State what God has revealed that you must admit responsibility for doing.

State what particular action(s) you will take today to accomplish what God has revealed for you to do.

Discovering the Discipline: Pursuing Service

For the next twelve weeks, we will commit ourselves to pursuing ways that we can serve Jesus within the ministry of the local church that we attend. Now, I fully understand that you may already be involved serving in some capacity at your local church. Be assured, there is no intention that you should stop performing the services that you provide. Rather, we will use these next weeks to resubmit whatever we are doing in service to the local church for the Lord's inspection and evaluation. By doing this we are asking Him to speak to us regarding how we may best serve Him. It is likely that He will direct you to continue in your current manner of serving. If that is the case, He will likely direct you to make some changes to how you conduct your ministering. These changes in your ministry and in yourself will stretch and grow your ability to serve Him. If you are not currently providing some regular service to your local church, you will use this time to ask the Lord how He intends for you to serve Him in your local church.

To help you in your inquiry, you will use the spiritual practices of prayer and fasting to aid in seeking after the Lord's direction. So, beginning today, you will prepare for a fast that will begin on Day One of Week Two in this book by establishing the *purpose* of your fasting.

Doing the Discipline: Preparing for a Fast
Determining the Purpose of My Fast

Today we begin to prepare for a fast that will begin on the morning of Day One of Week Two. Today you will establish the purpose for the fast. Normally, you would use the following steps to help you *determine* the purpose of your fast. However, as was said above, you will use this time of prayer and fasting to seek the Lord's direction concerning how He wants you to serve Him in your local church. Use the following steps to help you prepare for your fast.

1. Pray that God will guide you as you prepare yourself for a time of intense inspection, confession, adoration, revelation, and dedication.

2. Write a paragraph in the space below that describes what you want to be the outcome of your fast. Clearly state what you want to know from Him, about the way He wants you to serve Him and about what in particular He wants done by you to minister to others within your local church. State what you intend to do with this knowledge, or, in other words, how you will use what He reveals to accomplish His will.

The purpose of my fast, the issue upon which I will focus and about which I will ask God's direction is:

Journal

Record ideas, impressions, feelings, questions, and any insights you may have had during today's time.

Prayer

Pray for each member of your community.

Call to Ministry

DAY TWO

Prayer

Dear Lord, I realize that I lack so much in serving others. I don't do it enough (I don't even think about it very often), and I often lack the skills and resources necessary to meet their needs. Lord, make me able to serve other people with the supernatural power and desire only You can give. Amen.

Core Thought

Jesus calls us to serve one another in a supernatural way.

Most of us are very self-conscious. We tend to think a great deal about how things affect us. For example, I (Bill) often have trouble getting into worship at public gatherings because I can focus only on what I'm doing and what I look like to those around me. I am overly concerned with what I am doing and with what others might be thinking about me. This self-attention is natural, that is, it is automatic; I don't have to remind myself to be this way. Because I am like this, thinking first and foremost about others and what I can do to benefit them is not my normal way. Instead, it *feels* unnatural.

The act of loving others sacrificially is unnatural. The very notion of doing for others when it will cost us and we will not gain some advantage seems contrary to our normal way of thinking. It is so contrary that most of us also avoid moving into anything that looks like failure or might include suffering. This was never more evident than when Jesus told His followers that He was about to be killed, that it would be painful on many levels, and that everyone would be embarrassed.

On this occasion, He took the Twelve aside and told them what was going to happen to Him. "We are going up to Jerusalem," He said, "and the Son of Man will be betrayed to the chief priests and teachers of the law. They will condemn him to death and will hand him over to the Gentiles, who will mock him and spit on him, flog him and kill him" (Mark 10:33-34).

Imagine hearing these words today. We might think they sound pessimistic or that they lack the kind of faith we think we need—faith that wins the day or avoids trouble and shame. But Jesus led with weakness, failure, and rejection. He moved straight into everything that the human spirit naturally abhors. We will never minister from our natural character. Only out of a supernaturally empowered self-sacrificing character will there arise the attitude of willingness that is our rite of passage to ministering.

To minister as Jesus ministered is to serve with the supernatural freedom of self-sacrifice, to give ourselves for others. As an associate of Mother Teresa once commented, "She is free to be nothing; therefore, God can use her for anything."[1]

Today's Exercises

Core Scripture: 2 Corinthians 2 and 3
Read aloud 2 Corinthians 2:14-17; 3:4-6,17-18.
Recite this week's memory verse aloud five times.

> He has made us competent as ministers of a new covenant—not of the letter but of the Spirit; for the letter kills, but the Spirit gives life. (2 Corinthians 3:6)

Meditate on today's passage.

---

1. Bill Hull, *Complete Book of Discipleship: On Being and Making Followers of Christ* (Colorado Springs: NavPress, 2006), 144–146.

Request to Be in His Presence

"Dear Lord, bring me into the context of Your world."

1. ***Read it***—Remember: We read now only what is there, to hear once again, only what was spoken then. Read 1 Peter 1:2 at least twice, out loud.

2. ***Think it***—select a portion, a phrase within the reading, and mull mull it over in your mind, thinking about the context and setting, reimagining the event, putting yourself into the situation. As you meditate, use all five senses to re-create the context and the setting by building the images that are supplied within the passages.

3. ***Pray it***—ask God to give you understanding into how the truths He has spoken in these Scriptures apply to you now. Ask, "What is it about me that I need to deal with? What is it about me that must change?"

    Respond to God by accepting and admitting whatever responsibility is implied by what He has shown. Write what it is that God has shown you, and what you must admit responsibility for having done (or not done).

4. ***Live it***—ask God to reveal to you what He wants you to do about what you have admitted.

State what God has revealed that you must admit responsibility for doing.

State what particular action(s) you will take today to accomplish what God has revealed for you to do.

Doing the Discipline: Preparing for a Fast
Dedicating My Physical Self to God

Today you will dedicate your physical self, your body and its feelings and actions, as a living sacrifice to God in preparation for your time of fasting.

Keeping your purpose in mind, write a prayer dedicating your body, its strength, health, and comfort as a sacrifice to God. Acknowledge that He is the one who provides for your body, and state what it is that He provides for it. Tell Him why you are giving Him this time of fasting, that you give it freely whether your purpose is fulfilled or not, and that what you desire more than the fulfilling of your purpose is to enjoy this time in His presence.

My Prayer of Dedication to You, Lord:

Journal

Record ideas, impressions, feelings, questions, and any insights you may have had during today's time.

Prayer

Pray for each member of your community.

Call to Ministry

DAY THREE

Prayer

Dear Lord, help me not to withhold my service when You are directing me to minister to others. Train me not to ignore Your calling, especially when I may feel inadequate or unqualified to serve You. Amen.

Core Thought

> Jesus commands His ministers to be
> servants and calls only servants to His ministry.

Our English translations of the New Testament use the words *minister* and *servant* to translate the eight Greek words the New Testament writers used to capture the fullness of what it means to minister or serve in Jesus' name. We ought to realize that when two words are made to do the work of many there is bound to be something lost in the translation. To have a fuller understanding of what it means to minister and serve requires that we know the essence of what those Greek words were meant to convey. Relax, we are not going to study all eight. We look for essence, not exhaustion.

The first and most often used of these words is δουλο (*doulos*). It is the word for slave or bond-servant and is used to emphasize the lowliness of Christian service. It is also used metaphorically to indicate the attitude that Christ's disciples will display, one of devotion to another disregarding of one's own interests. It was the kind of servant Jesus became, the form of a bond-servant that Christ assumed (Philippians 2:7). Following His example, it is this kind of servant, a slave, the *doulos* of God (or Christ), that the apostles, their fellow-laborers, and we are called to be (Romans 1:1; Galatians 1:10; Colossians 4:12; Titus 1:1; James 1:1; 2 Peter 1:1).

No matter what nuances might be contained within the words for servant, what cannot be ignored is that they all insist that one idea is primary: A servant is someone who actually performs the tasks whole-heartedly himself. Inherent in the word itself is the disclaimer against any disciple of Jesus proclaiming themselves to be only a big-picture man and not a worker bee. The very word *servant* declares that all disciples will be found ministering (working, serving) with their own hands (Ephesians 4:28; 1 Thessalonians 4:11). The meaning of servant includes ministering in all kinds of ways, but it excludes any notion of different classes of servants.

To minister as Jesus ministered means to minister to others whole-heartedly as their personal servant.

Today's Exercises

Core Scripture: 2 Corinthians 2 and 3

Read aloud 2 Corinthians 2:14-17; 3:4-6,17-18.

Recite this week's memory verse aloud five times.

> He has made us competent as ministers of a new covenant—not of the letter but of the Spirit; for the letter kills, but the Spirit gives life. (2 Corinthians 3:6)

Meditate on today's passage.

Request to Be in His Presence

"Dear Lord, bring me into the context of Your world."

1. *Read it*—Remember: We read now only what is there, to hear once again, only what was spoken then. Read 1 Peter 1:3 at least twice, out loud.

2. *Think it*—select a portion, a phrase within the reading, and mull

mull it over in your mind, thinking about the context and setting, reimagining the event, putting yourself into the situation. As you meditate, use all five senses to re-create the context and the setting by building the images that are supplied within the passages.

3. ***Pray it***—ask God to give you understanding into how the truths He has spoken in these Scriptures apply to you now. Ask, "What is it about me that I need to deal with? What is it about me that must change?"

    Respond to God by accepting and admitting whatever responsibility is implied by what He has shown. Write what it is that God has shown you, and what you must admit responsibility for having done (or not done).

4. ***Live it***—ask God to reveal to you what He wants you to do about what you have admitted.

State what God has revealed that you must admit responsibility for doing.

State what particular action(s) you will take today to accomplish what God has revealed for you to do.

Doing the Discipline: Preparing for a Fast

Begin by reciting the prayer of dedication that you wrote yesterday.

Determining the Privation of My Fast

Today you will prepare for the fast by determining the *privation* of your fasting. You will align the privation of the fast with the purpose for your fasting. You will decide what it is in which you will de-*prive* yourself during your fast.

You may determine for example, that a five-day, one-meal, water-only fast such as the one you conducted in Book Two will do just fine and leave it at that. You may however be directed by the Lord to abstain from a very specific activity for the duration of the fast. For instance, if you are feeling anxious about having enough time to serve in your local church, you might decide to abstain from watching any television, playing video games, and Internet browsing for the duration of your fast, using the time instead for prayer and studying God's Word. You may decide to deprive yourself of two hours of sleep each day by waking early and using the time for prayer and studying God's Word.

In the space provided below, write down what you will deprive yourself of for the period (or duration) of your fast:

For the duration of my fast, I will deprive myself of

Journal

Record ideas, impressions, feelings, questions, and any insights you may have had during today's time.

Prayer

Pray for each member of your community.

Call to Ministry

DAY FOUR

Prayer

Dear Lord, I don't like being hailed as some sort of Christian leader. I am not comfortable being in the limelight. Please teach me to get used to being uncomfortable. Train me to care less and less about how others see me and more about making sure others see more and more of You when they see me. Amen.

Core Thought

> Jesus calls His disciples to minister as ambassadors.

Before we can talk about loving as Jesus loved, we had better make sure we know what we mean by love. The word translated as *minister* is διακουο *(diakonos)*. To Greek-speaking society in the apostle Paul's day, it was the title conferred upon the person who carried out the assignments and tasks given to him by a kingdom's ambassador.

The word for ambassador, πρεσβευω *(presbeuō)*, conveys two ideas: an elderly seasoned leader and an appointed representative. An ambassador was an experienced representative appointed by a king to advance his kingdom's interests in a foreign land. The ambassador leads a delegation, the king's envoy, into another kingdom. There he establishes and directs the mission of his king's embassy *(presbeia)*. The work of the king's embassy is performed by the embassy's ministers *(diakonos)*.

The minister performs the work that is necessary to accomplish an ambassador's mission. A minister's primary duties were to promote loyalty to the king among his subjects, secure the allegiance of rebelling subjects, and deliver the king's beneficence according to his commands.

The apostle Paul uses the meaning behind the words *minister* and *ambassador* to convey what it means to minister in Jesus' name. Paul describes himself as an "ambassador for Christ" (Ephesians 6:20). While Christ appoints different gifts to believers for building up the church (Ephesians 4:11-16), all believers are ministers, laymen, one of many who worship and serve at their local church, responsible for bringing the King's message to the people. According to Paul, "anyone [who] is in Christ" is commissioned (called, appointed) by the King as His minister with the King's full power (2 Corinthians 5:17-18).

To minister as Jesus ministered is to serve as God's appointed minister of reconciliation, serving our brothers and sisters in Christ, encouraging their faithfulness, and calling the rebellious to surrender their allegiance to Jesus, the King of Kings.

Today's Exercises
Core Scripture: 2 Corinthians 2 and 3
Read aloud 2 Corinthians 2:14-17; 3:4-6,17-18.
Recite this week's memory verse aloud five times.

> He has made us competent as ministers of a new covenant— not of the letter but of the Spirit; for the letter kills, but the Spirit gives life. (2 Corinthians 3:6)

Meditate on today's passage.

Request to Be in His Presence
"Dear Lord, bring me into the context of Your world."

1. **Read it**—Remember: We read now only what is there, to hear once again, only what was spoken then. Read 1 Peter 1:4-5 at least twice, out loud.
2. **Think it**—select a portion, a phrase within the reading, and mull it over in your mind, thinking about the context and setting,

reimagining the event, putting yourself into the situation. As you meditate, use all five senses to re-create the context and the setting by building the images that are supplied within the passages.

3. *Pray it*—ask God to give you understanding into how the truths He has spoken in these Scriptures apply to you now. Ask, "What is it about me that I need to deal with? What is it about me that must change?"

Respond to God by accepting and admitting whatever responsibility is implied by what He has shown. Write what it is that God has shown you, and what you must admit responsibility for having done (or not done).

4. *Live it*—ask God to reveal to you what He wants you to do about what you have admitted.

State what God has revealed that you must admit responsibility for doing.

State what particular action(s) you will take today to accomplish what God has revealed for you to do.

Doing the Discipline: Preparing for a Fast
Begin by reciting your prayer of dedication.

Determining the Period of My Fasting
Today you will establish the *period* of your fasting, the duration of your fast. You will align the period or duration of your fast with the purpose for your fasting. We recommend (unless the Lord leads you otherwise) that you engage in a five-day fast.

If you are going to engage in a fast of a different duration, we offer the following as guidelines to help you.

- The period of any fast should be long enough to allow you to experience the full range of uncomfortable feelings that will come from depriving yourself.
- The period of any fast should not be so short that it will be ineffective in revealing anything to you. If it is so short that it will not cause you to "raise a sweat," it is too short to capture your attention and too short a workout to strengthen you.
- The period of any fast should be long enough for you to be able to stay focused on the presence of God, to hear *His* voice instead of attending to the cravings and ravings of your body. It will challenge and serve to reveal the current content of your character. If the period of your fasting is sufficient, it will allow a heightened spiritual awareness of being in God's presence, and being in the light of the nearness of His presence will always result in the revealing of the condition of your own heart.
- The period of any fast should not be so long that it will cause others to suffer or be deprived of the services that we ought to be providing to them.

In the space provided below, write down the period (or duration) of your fast:

The duration of my fast will be: _____ days.

Journal

Record ideas, impressions, feelings, questions, and any insights you may have had during today's time.

Prayer

Pray for each member of your community.

Call to Ministry

DAY FIVE

Prayer

Dear Lord, help me to be able to serve anyone to whom You call me to minister. Train me not to prequalify them for Your love. Help me to present Your selfless love for them through the service You call me to give them in Your name. Amen.

Core Thought

> Jesus calls His ministers to serve three kinds of people.

There are three kinds of people who are served by Jesus' ministers: people who are enlisted, people who are enslaved, and people who are exiled.

First, Jesus calls His ministers to serve the people who are currently enlisted in serving Him. These are the loyal believers and our fellow-laborers. They are citizens of Jesus' kingdom who are serving Him where they live, work, play, and worship. We are to serve these brothers and sisters in Christ by encouraging them in the work of their ministry, supplying their needs, and praying for their faithfulness. We are to love them as devotedly as Jesus loved us.

Secondly, we are to minister to the enslaved. These are citizens of Jesus' kingdom that have been taken captive by the enemy. They are believers who have fallen back under the influence of the kingdom of darkness. They are sin-sick and have become beguiled by this kingdom's prince, the devil. Our ministry to them is one of rescue and recovery. We minister to them by coming to their rescue and aiding them to break the bondage they have forged from engaging in sinful behavior. We serve them by helping them to recover the freedom in Christ they enjoyed before their bondage made it intolerable. We offer them accountability in an environment of grace and honesty and integrity in a relationship of trust.

Thirdly, Jesus' ministers are called to serve the people who are refugees, the excluded. These are those who are not yet citizens of Jesus' kingdom. They have been marked as valueless by this world and are cast aside. They are the poor, hungry, and homeless, the victims of injustice and the target of exploitation by this world's system. They are the despised who wander the land, seeking rest and a home, but remain restless, tired, and homeless. They are those who "have ears to hear" and will follow when Jesus bids them, "Come to me, all you who are weary and burdened, and I will give you rest. Take my yoke upon you and learn from me, for I am gentle and humble in heart, and you will find rest for your souls. For my yoke is easy and my burden is light" (Matthew 11:28-30).

Today's Exercises
Core Scripture: 2 Corinthians 2 and 3
Read aloud 2 Corinthians 2:14-17; 3:4-6,17-18.
Recite this week's memory verse aloud five times.

> He has made us competent as ministers of a new covenant—not of the letter but of the Spirit; for the letter kills, but the Spirit gives life. (2 Corinthians 3:6)

Meditate on today's passage.

Request to Be in His Presence
"Dear Lord, bring me into the context of Your world."

1. ***Read it***—Remember: We read now only what is there, to hear once again, only what was spoken then. Read 1 Peter 1:6 at least twice, out loud.

2. ***Think it***—select a portion, a phrase within the reading, and mull it over in your mind, thinking about the context and setting, reimagining the event, putting yourself into the situation. As you meditate, use all five senses to re-create the context and the setting by building the images that are supplied within the passages.

3. ***Pray it***—ask God to give you understanding into how the truths He has spoken in these Scriptures apply to you now. Ask, "What is it about me that I need to deal with? What is it about me that must change?"

   Respond to God by accepting and admitting whatever responsibility is implied by what He has shown. Write what it is that God has shown you, and what you must admit responsibility for having done (or not done).

4. ***Live it***—ask God to reveal to you what He wants you to do about what you have admitted.

State what God has revealed that you must admit responsibility for doing.

State what particular action(s) you will take today to accomplish what God has revealed for you to do.

Doing the Discipline: Preparing for a Fast

Begin by reciting your prayer of dedication.

Directing My Spirit's Passions Toward God

Today you will begin to direct your spirit's passion toward God in preparation for your fast.

Pray, asking God to direct your passions toward Him

Ask Him to guide you during this journey of making His will the main passion in your life, and to help you trust in Him as He shows you His way to accomplish His will.

Journal

Record ideas, impressions, feelings, questions, and any insights you may have had during today's time.

Prayer

Pray for each member of your community.

Call to Ministry

DAY SIX

Community Meeting

In preparation for this week's meeting, you will have read and reflected upon each of the week's five Core Thoughts, recorded your thoughts and observations, and are ready to recite this week's memory verse to the group.

WEEK TWO

Commitment to Ministry

DAY ONE

Prayer

Dear Jesus, I've always been resistant to making commitments. I never want to let anyone down if I can't keep my commitment. Teach me not to fear making and keeping my commitments with You. Train me to trust in Your ability to make me succeed, no matter what that success may look like to others. Amen.

Core Thought

> High commitment to ministry is required of all who minister in Jesus' name.

High commitment is a message for the multitudes. That means it's for everyone. There are several high-commitment passages that support this thesis. In Luke 9:23-25, 9:57-62, and 14:26, high commitment is for "anyone who would follow me" or "come after me." The teaching of Luke 9:57-62 springs from a statement made by an unidentified man along the road. While the 9:23-25 passage setting only involves the Twelve, the teaching is for "anyone" and is consistent with Jesus' other requirements for following Him. Jesus is telling us that while many of today's evangelical Christians may be Christians, they are less Christian than He requires.

While it is a message for everyone, in all candor we must admit that only a few make high commitment a practiced reality. A simple example is the expectation that every disciple is to faithfully represent Christ in our culture in both word and deed.

Jesus demonstrated the power and the price of not retreating from the value of high commitment. He wept over an unresponsive Jerusalem, but He didn't allow His emotions to cloud His judgment. Once people heard the message, He invited them to follow. If they chose not to, He didn't lower the requirements, for it is not loving to mislead followers into the false belief that superficial spirituality will be rewarded by God. Several months after Jesus had chosen the Twelve to "be with him" (Mark 3:14) and only a few months before the cross, there was a confrontation at Capernaum concerning commitment. Confronted by the religious establishment's representatives, Jesus told them He was the "bread of life" and "no one can come to me unless the Father . . . draws him, and I will raise him up at the last day" (John 6:35-51). Of course, these comments were blasphemous to the Jewish leaders, and no one was surprised by their displeasure. But then Jesus told them, "I tell you the truth, unless you eat the flesh of the Son of Man and drink his blood, you have no life in you. Whoever eats my flesh and drinks my blood has eternal life, and I will raise him up at the last day. For my flesh is real food and my blood is real drink. Whoever eats my flesh and drinks my blood remains in me, and I in him" (John 6:53-56). The Pharisees were appalled, and the disciples were scared. Jesus was locked in a conflict where the stakes were high. His followers were disoriented, even shocked.

It is expected that the unbelieving world, both religious and secular, will oppose the clear, unyielding Christian message. Unyielding refers to accepting the total package, including Jesus being the only way to God and eternal punishment in a real place called hell. The message scandalizes the syncretistic world, and many Christians wilt in the heat of its demands. Such claims of absolute truth and the knowledge of the narrow way prescribed by Jesus offend the unregenerate mind. The non-Christian mind longs for an easy answer that allows plenty of moral wiggle room. Secular society's greatest sin is intolerance; the Christian's greatest sin is insubordination. That is why one of the last things Jesus told His followers was that the world would reject the message and hate the messengers (John 15:18-21; 16:33).

This conflict teaches us that many who say, "I am a Christian," are exposed for who they really are when the chips are down. Even in light of all our good theological systems, much the same thing happens today when Christians are confronted with the full range of Jesus' demands on their lives.[1]

Today's Exercises

Core Scripture: 2 Corinthians 4:1-5,10

Read aloud 2 Corinthians 4:1-5,10.

Recite this week's memory verses aloud five times.

> Brothers, I do not consider myself yet to have taken hold of it. But one thing I do: Forgetting what is behind and straining toward what is ahead, I press on toward the goal to win the prize for which God has called me heavenward in Christ Jesus. (Philippians 3:13-14)

Meditate on today's passage.

Request to Be in His Presence

"Dear Lord, bring me into the context of Your world."

1. *Read it*—Remember: We read now only what is there, to hear once again, only what was spoken then. Read 1 Peter 1:7 at least twice, out loud.
2. *Think it*—select a portion, a phrase within the reading, and mull it over in your mind, thinking about the context and setting, reimagining the event, putting yourself into the situation. As you meditate, use all five senses to re-create the context and the setting by building the images that are supplied within the passages.

---

1. Bill Hull, *Building High Commitment in a Low-Commitment World.* (Grand Rapids: Fleming H. Revell, 1995), 128–134.

3. *Pray it*—ask God to give you understanding into how the truths He has spoken in these Scriptures apply to you now. Ask, "What is it about me that I need to deal with? What is it about me that must change?"

   Respond to God by accepting and admitting whatever responsibility is implied by what He has shown. Write what it is that God has shown you, and what you must admit responsibility for having done (or not done).

4. *Live it*—ask God to reveal to you what He wants you to do about what you have admitted.

   State what God has revealed that you must admit responsibility for doing.

   State what particular action(s) you will take today to accomplish what God has revealed for you to do.

Doing the Discipline: Executing Your Fast

If you are doing the recommended fast:

Beginning with today's first meal and continuing until the evening meal of Day Five, you will abstain from eating the first and second meals of the day. You may eat your evening or last meal of the day as usual, but you are to skip the morning and midday meals. During the entirety of the fast you may drink water at any time. You will break your fast with "break-fast" the morning of Day Six of this week.

- Pray at the beginning of each day of the fast by reciting the prayer of dedication that you wrote on Day Two of last week.
- Pray again that God would direct your spirit's passion toward Him.
- Remember to keep a journal of your experiences during your fast.

If you are doing a fast of a different kind:

- Note how the special design of your fast is helping you to accomplish the purpose of your fast.

Journal

Record ideas, impressions, feelings, questions, and any insights you may have had during today's time.

Prayer

Pray for each member of your community.

Commitment to Ministry

DAY TWO

Prayer

Dear Lord, I always want others to be truthful with me. At least most of the time. I guess what I really mean is that I like the truth when it is what I want to hear. Train me, Lord, to be known by others as someone who uncompromisingly conducts themselves truthfully and graciously. Amen.

Core Thought

Commitment to ministry is high commitment to truth.

Revulsion in the face of Christian truth is not the exclusive right of unbelievers. Many evangelicals can't stomach some of Jesus' teachings either. Even some of those following Jesus in His day decided that the requirements were unrealistic. "On hearing it, many of his disciples said, 'This is a hard teaching. Who can accept it?'" (John 6:60). Jesus' response was not to do the contemporary theological backstroke, lowering the heat in order to keep His followers in tow. He told them what He taught was truth and that their response might be an evidence that they really didn't believe. Although they had gotten captured by the excitement, when things got difficult, they were not with Him.

The sad result was the departure of many of His followers. It comes as somewhat of a surprise that Jesus didn't say, "If you change your mind, come on back." Jesus didn't run after those who rejected His teaching. A bigger surprise was His immediate comment to the Twelve. He didn't say, "Whew! I'm sure glad you guys are sticking with Me. Without you, there would be no way to finish the task, and I would need to start over." Instead He demonstrated the importance of truth over personnel by saying, "You do not want to leave too, do you?" (John 6:67). This was their best chance to opt out of what they knew would be a risky future.

Say what you will about the foibles of this suspect band of disciples, but at least, in most cases, they hung in there and stayed committed. The clear lesson is that those who are committed to Jesus stay, and they stay because they have tasted the reality of God. Anything less is not worth living for. "Simon Peter answered him. 'Lord, to whom shall we go? You have the words of eternal life. We believe and know that you are the Holy One of God'" (verses 68-69). True believers are committed to the Truth.[2]

Today's Exercises

Core Scripture: 2 Corinthians 4:1-5,10

Read aloud 2 Corinthians 4:1-5,10.

Recite this week's memory verses aloud five times.

> Brothers, I do not consider myself yet to have taken hold of it.
> But one thing I do: Forgetting what is behind and straining
> toward what is ahead, I press on toward the goal to win the
> prize for which God has called me heavenward in Christ Jesus.
> (Philippians 3:13-14)

Meditate on today's passage.

Request to Be in His Presence

"Dear Lord, bring me into the context of Your world."

1. *Read it*—Remember: We read now only what is there, to hear once again, only what was spoken then. Read 1 Peter 1:8-9 at least twice, out loud.

---

2. Hull, *Building High Commitment*, 133–134.

2. *Think it*—select a portion, a phrase within the reading, and mull it over in your mind, thinking about the context and setting, reimagining the event, putting yourself into the situation. As you meditate, use all five senses to re-create the context and the setting by building the images that are supplied within the passages.

3. *Pray it*—ask God to give you understanding into how the truths He has spoken in these Scriptures apply to you now. Ask, "What is it about me that I need to deal with? What is it about me that must change?"

   Respond to God by accepting and admitting whatever responsibility is implied by what He has shown. Write what it is that God has shown you, and what you must admit responsibility for having done (or not done).

4. *Live it*—ask God to reveal to you what He wants you to do about what you have admitted.

State what God has revealed that you must admit responsibility for doing.

State what particular action(s) you will take today to accomplish what God has revealed for you to do.

Doing the Discipline: Continuing Your Fast

- Pray, at the beginning of each day of the fast, by reciting the prayer of dedication that you wrote on Day Two of last week.
- Pray again that God would direct your spirit's passion toward Him.

Documenting My Perspective During My Fasting

- Remember to keep a journal of your experiences during your fast.
- Note how the special design of your fast is helping you to accomplish the purpose of your fast.

Journal

Record ideas, impressions, feelings, questions, and any insights you may have had during today's time.

Prayer

Pray for each member of your community.

Commitment to Ministry

DAY THREE

Prayer

Father, thank You for being absolutely committed to transforming me into one whose character will overflow with the same love and faithfulness that Jesus has shown. Amen.

Core Thought

Commitment to ministry is high commitment to faithfulness.

Faithfulness is the rite of passage to any meaningful Christian experience. Various clubs and organizations have their entry-level traditions that make it possible for new members to adhere and to advance. The Israeli army requires all soldiers to run up the historic Masada at night with a torch in hand. They stand in the darkness above the Dead Sea and sing their national anthem. Athletic teams engage in mild forms of hazing to initiate their rookies. There always seems to be some hurdle for the new member to clear. You will be glad to know there is no evangelical hazing; there is, however, a basic entry-level requirement for ministering in Jesus' name—faithfulness.

Paul taught and practiced this rite of passage. Paul called Christian ministry a responsibility, a service (1 Timothy 3:10), a trust (1 Corinthians 4:2), and Jesus referred to this responsibility as "true riches" (Luke 16:11). He taught that before someone is to be entrusted with ministering to others in Jesus' name, he must first prove to others that he is faithful in obeying Jesus commands: "Now it is required that those who have been given a trust must prove faithful" (1 Corinthians

4:2). There is no expectation of perfection in what is being taught, but Jesus looks for a pattern of behavior establishing that one can be trusted to keep their commitments to God and to others. After providing Timothy with a long list of character qualities, Paul also includes that those who are being considered to minister to others "must first be tested; *and then if there is nothing against them*, let them serve as deacons" (or ministers, literally 'serve as servants,' 1 Timothy 3:10, emphasis added). Not only did Paul teach that faithfulness was basic entry-level commitment, he cautioned against giving the unfaithful anything valuable: "And the things you have heard me say in the presence of many witnesses entrust to *reliable* men who will also be qualified to teach others" (2 Timothy 2:2).[3]

The plain and simple theme is that proving one's self faithful is the prelude to ministry. To minister as Jesus ministered we must submit to having our trustworthiness proven by being tested by others, and having our faithfulness established by being attested to by others.

Today's Exercises
Core Scripture: 2 Corinthians 4:1-5,10
Read aloud 2 Corinthians 4:1-5,10.
Recite this week's memory verses aloud five times.

> Brothers, I do not consider myself yet to have taken hold of it. But one thing I do: Forgetting what is behind and straining toward what is ahead, I press on toward the goal to win the prize for which God has called me heavenward in Christ Jesus. (Philippians 3:13-14)

Meditate on today's passage.

Request to Be in His Presence
> *"Dear Lord, bring me into the context of Your world."*

---

3. Hull, *Building High Commitment*, 140–142.

1. ***Read it***—Remember: We read now only what is there, to hear once again, only what was spoken then. Read 1 Peter 1:10-11 at least twice, out loud.

2. ***Think it***—select a portion, a phrase within the reading, and mull it over in your mind, thinking about the context and setting, reimagining the event, putting yourself into the situation. As you meditate, use all five senses to re-create the context and the setting by building the images that are supplied within the passages.

3. ***Pray it***—ask God to give you understanding into how the truths He has spoken in these Scriptures apply to you now. Ask, "What is it about me that I need to deal with? What is it about me that must change?"

   Respond to God by accepting and admitting whatever responsibility is implied by what He has shown. Write what it is that God has shown you, and what you must admit responsibility for having done (or not done).

4. ***Live it***—ask God to reveal to you what He wants you to do about what you have admitted.

State what God has revealed that you must admit responsibility for doing.

State what particular action(s) you will take today to accomplish what God has revealed for you to do.

Doing the Discipline: Continuing Your Fast

- Pray, at the beginning of each day of the fast, by reciting the prayer of dedication that you wrote on Day Two of last week.
- Pray again that God would direct your spirit's passion toward Him.

Documenting My Perspective During My Fasting

- Remember to keep a journal of your experiences during your fast.
- Note how the special design of your fast is helping you to accomplish the purpose of your fast.

Journal

Record ideas, impressions, feelings, questions, and any insights you may have had during today's time.

Prayer

Pray for each member of your community.

Commitment to Ministry

DAY FOUR

Prayer

Dear Lord, show me the things about myself that keep me from freely serving You anytime, anywhere, and any way You may be calling me. Train me to overcome these things by living consistently in the power of your Spirit. Amen.

Core Thought

> Commitment to ministry means committing
> with others to overcome our barriers to obedience.

Church is like a group of people standing in a large field, all trying to move in the same direction. At one end of the field is the goal, Christlikeness. People are standing at various stages of the journey: Some have made good progress, others very little, most are somewhere in the middle. Most are not moving because they all stand in front of a very high barrier that they can't seem to get over on their own. This barrier is personal and different for each individual. These are obedience barriers, the sins or difficulties that continue to dominate their lives. All of us have the besetting sins, the chronic sins that are our weaknesses. It seems as if every time we start making good progress, we get blocked by our chronic sin.

Obedience barriers are varied and almost always camouflaged. One leader told me he was too busy to serve as an elder. He claimed he was overworked and overcommitted and that serving would require too much of him. All he knew was that he was out of time and money.

But I knew the issues were deeper. A few weeks later he told me of his ongoing affair with a woman at work; the guilt and emotional turmoil at home made it impossible for him to serve.

If we had known of his marital issues and his struggle in the workplace, someone could have helped him over that obedience barrier. But for this to happen the Christian needs to grant those around him two things: proximity and permission. Proximity means regular access to him so that they can get to know him well and establish trust. Permission means that once trust is developed, he grants permission for someone to enter his life and to talk about the real issues. This is accountability in community.

Without accountability you can't make disciples. Accountability is helping others keep their commitments to God. There are no exceptions to the rule that we need others' help in making our spiritual journey as productive as possible. If people could read the Bible or hear a message and then go out and live the Christian life without encouragement, correction, or discipline, we would need only Bibles, but not churches. Any casual observer of human behavior knows how naive such a belief actually is. Few among us — there may be none — haven't needed someone to come along and help us over an obedience barrier (or two or three hundred) during our lives.

When obedience barriers are not being dealt with and there is no participation in a community to provide the necessary accountability to root out emotional and spiritual pathology, we will carry these pathologies into our areas of ministry and, just as tragically, into our own family life.[4]

Today's Exercises

Core Scripture: 2 Corinthians 4:1-5,10
Read aloud 2 Corinthians 4:1-5,10.
Recite this week's memory verses aloud five times.

---

4. Hull, *Building High Commitment*, 146–148.

Brothers, I do not consider myself yet to have taken hold of it. But one thing I do: Forgetting what is behind and straining toward what is ahead, I press on toward the goal to win the prize for which God has called me heavenward in Christ Jesus. (Philippians 3:13-14)

Meditate on today's passage.

Request to Be in His Presence

"Dear Lord, bring me into the context of Your world."

1. *Read it*—Remember: We read now only what is there, to hear once again, only what was spoken then. Read 1 Peter 1:12 at least twice, out loud.
2. *Think it*—select a portion, a phrase within the reading, and mull it over in your mind, thinking about the context and setting, reimagining the event, putting yourself into the situation. As you meditate, use all five senses to re-create the context and the setting by building the images that are supplied within the passages.
3. *Pray it*—ask God to give you understanding into how the truths He has spoken in these Scriptures apply to you now. Ask, "What is it about me that I need to deal with? What is it about me that must change?"

    Respond to God by accepting and admitting whatever responsibility is implied by what He has shown. Write what it is that God has shown you, and what you must admit responsibility for having done (or not done).
4. *Live it*—ask God to reveal to you what He wants you to do about what you have admitted.

State what God has revealed that you must admit responsibility for doing.

State what particular action(s) you will take today to accomplish what God has revealed for you to do.

Doing the Discipline: Continuing Your Fast

- Pray at the beginning of each day of the fast by reciting the prayer of dedication that you wrote on Day Two of last week.
- Pray again that God would direct your spirit's passion toward Him.

Documenting My Perspective During My Fasting

- Remember to keep a journal of your experiences during your fast.
- Note how the special design of your fast is helping you to accomplish the purpose of your fast.

Journal

Record ideas, impressions, feelings, questions, and any insights you may have had during today's time.

Prayer

Pray for each member of your community.

Commitment to Ministry

DAY FIVE

Prayer

Dear Father, it's remarkable to think that You consider me to be a member of Your family and that You have entrusted the conducting of our family's business to me. I know it's way beyond my ability. Thank You for partnering me with Jesus. With Your Spirit's direction I know I can be successful. Please help me and my other brothers and sisters to do our business Your way. Amen.

Core Thought

> Commitment to ministry is establishing a high-commitment partnership doing the Father's business.

The important thing for a servant to learn is what his master requires him to do and the way his master requires that it be done. The essential characteristic of a trusted servant is his faithfulness in accomplishing his master's will his master's way. The ultimate goal for any servant is to become a full partner in his master's business. Jesus said, "I no longer call you servants, because a servant does not know his master's business. Instead, I have called you friends, for everything that I learned from my Father I have made known to you" (John 15:14-15).

For Christians, ministering in Jesus' name is the way we become full partners with Jesus as He accomplishes His Father's business. As with any business, we must acquire the knowledge, skills, temperament, and proficiency to competently conduct the Father's business before we can serve as a partner with Jesus in the family business. To gain this competency we must enter into apprenticeship with Jesus, become His apprentice in ministry.

To apprentice with Jesus in ministry means that we not only commit and do regular ministry but also that we begin a dedicated course of study to gain a deeper understanding of all that ministering with Jesus entails. We must learn our life's purpose, how we fit into the larger drama of God's redemptive plan, and what service our individual ministry contributes to the mission of the local church. As apprentices, we must begin to upgrade our biblical/philosophical understanding of the Church and its mission, and more specifically the local church's mission and our responsibilities to it. We must train ourselves to keep the larger good of the church in mind. We will continue to gain crucial experiential knowledge about ministry by remaining active in our personal ministries, but we must not rely on these experiences to provide us with the well-rounded theology and personal and corporate philosophy of ministry necessary for us to be a full partner in Jesus' ministry.[5]

To minister as Jesus ministered means that we are highly committed to doing our part in accomplishing the Father's business of reconciling the world to Himself by ministering to others in Jesus' name.

Today's Exercises

Core Scripture: 2 Corinthians 4:1-5,10
Read aloud 2 Corinthians 4:1-5,10.
Recite this week's memory verses aloud five times.

> Brothers, I do not consider myself yet to have taken hold of it. But one thing I do: Forgetting what is behind and straining toward what is ahead, I press on toward the goal to win the prize for which God has called me heavenward in Christ Jesus. (Philippians 3:13-14)

---

5. Hull, *Building High Commitment*, 152–153.

Meditate on today's passage.

Request to Be in His Presence

"Dear Lord, bring me into the context of Your world."

1. ***Read it***—Remember: We read now only what is there, to hear once again, only what was spoken then. Read 1 Peter 1:13 at least twice, out loud.

2. ***Think it***—select a portion, a phrase within the reading, and mull it over in your mind, thinking about the context and setting, reimagining the event, putting yourself into the situation. As you meditate, use all five senses to re-create the context and the setting by building the images that are supplied within the passages.

3. ***Pray it***—ask God to give you understanding into how the truths He has spoken in these Scriptures apply to you now. Ask, "What is it about me that I need to deal with? What is it about me that must change?"

   Respond to God by accepting and admitting whatever responsibility is implied by what He has shown. Write what it is that God has shown you, and what you must admit responsibility for having done (or not done).

4. ***Live it***—ask God to reveal to you what He wants you to do about what you have admitted.

State what God has revealed that you must admit responsibility for doing.

State what particular action(s) you will take today to accomplish what God has revealed for you to do.

Documenting My Perspective During My Fasting

- Remember to keep a journal of your experiences during your fast.
- Note how the special design of your fast is helping you to accomplish the purpose of your fast.

Journal

Record ideas, impressions, feelings, questions, and any insights you may have had during today's time.

Prayer

Pray for each member of your community.

Commitment to Ministry

DAY SIX

Doing the Discipline: Breaking Your Fast
Deriving the Profit from My Fasting
Start by reviewing the journal entries that you made:

1. Read each statement and ask yourself, "What did I mean when I wrote this down?"
2. Using the space below, answer the questions:

"What did I experience?"

"What do I know now, from these experiences?"

3. Ask the Lord the following questions and write whatever comes to your mind as the result.

"Lord, what do you want me to learn from these experiences?"

"Lord, what do you want me to do with what I now know?"

4. Write a short summary of what you experienced while preparing, executing, and breaking your fast.

5. Write a short statement of what you learned and what you believe God is leading you to do with what you have learned from your fast about serving Him in your local church.

6. Go to your community meeting.

WEEK THREE

Conduct in Ministry

DAY ONE

Prayer

Father, I want to stay focused on serving others and serving them in ways that are pleasing to You. Please train me to respond to others as graciously as Jesus did by growing in me the same understanding and dedication to doing Your will as Jesus possessed. Amen.

Core Thought

> The integrity of our ministry is directly related to the extent to which Christ is being formed in us.

How we do ministry, how we serve others, is as important as *what* we do to serve others. What we do when we minister to someone and the way we do it are the chief means by which others experience the love of God. It is also the evidence that we truly believe the things we have said (1 John 4:7-16).

Integrity of ministry means that the service we give to others in Jesus' name is the natural consequence of our living obediently according to the truth revealed by God's Word. It means that my *general* understanding of what ministry to others is and in *general* how it must be conducted will be *formed* by what God's Spirit has revealed in His Word. It also means that my understanding as to what I am being called to do and the way I am to minister to any *particular* person must *conform* to the Word but must also be *informed* by the direction of the Holy Spirit.

The Holy Spirit directs and empowers all ministry that is done in Jesus' name. The Holy Spirit causes the life of Christ to be formed in us. As He is transforming us and our minds are being renewed, the Spirit is causing Christ's life to be lived through us. Our behaviors change from those commonly found in the world to those that reflect an uncommonly Christlike character. The more the Spirit transforms our likeness into Christ's, the more there will flow from His character growing in us acts of loving service in Jesus' name.

To minister as Jesus ministered requires that my beliefs and my behavior be transformed and integrated into a life of obedience to Jesus' commands by the power of His Spirit.

Today's Exercises

Core Scripture: 2 Corinthians 5:11-21

Read aloud 2 Corinthians 5:11-21.

Recite this week's memory verse aloud five times.

> Whatever happens, conduct yourselves in a manner worthy of the gospel of Christ. Then, whether I come and see you or only hear about you in my absence, I will know that you stand firm in one spirit, contending as one man for the faith of the gospel. (Philippians 1:27)

Meditate on today's passage.

Request to Be in His Presence

"Dear Lord, bring me into the context of Your world."

1. *Read it*—Remember: We read now only what is there, to hear once again, only what was spoken then. Read 1 Peter 1:14-16 at least twice, out loud.
2. *Think it*—select a portion, a phrase within the reading, and mull it over in your mind, thinking about the context and setting, reimagining the event, putting yourself into the situation. As you

meditate, use all five senses to re-create the context and the setting by building the images that are supplied within the passages.

3. *Pray it*—ask God to give you understanding into how the truths He has spoken in these Scriptures apply to you now. Ask, "What is it about me that I need to deal with? What is it about me that must change?"

Respond to God by accepting and admitting whatever responsibility is implied by what He has shown. Write what it is that God has shown you, and what you must admit responsibility for having done (or not done).

4. *Live it*—ask God to reveal to you what He wants you to do about what you have admitted.

State what God has revealed that you must admit responsibility for doing.

State what particular action(s) you will take today to accomplish what God has revealed for you to do.

Discovering the Discipline: Serving

Hopefully, your fast has resulted in your being led in some specific way to make changes in the way you serve in your local church. Perhaps it has resulted in your beginning to minister in a way or in an area of service you had not considered previously. It is possible (in fact it is most common) that after your five-day fast you may be as unclear or unsure as to what the Lord wants you to do as you were before you fasted. In other words, you're feeling like you haven't accomplished anything by fasting. If the latter is the case, do not fret. This week, we will continue to seek the Lord's guidance regarding how to serve Him in our local church. We will offer several approaches to help you discern the Lord's will in this matter.

Doing the Discipline

If the Lord has led you to begin serving Him in some specific way, for instance, to become active ministering to the college-age members of your church, then your goal this week is to discover what needs you can meet by serving within this ministry.

- Today, identify the ministry within your local church in which the Lord is leading you to serve. Write it in the space provided here. _____
- Continue to pray, specifically asking the Lord to show you how He wants you to serve *within this ministry* and how you can meet the needs He wants you to meet.
- Tomorrow, we will continue to discover what specifically the Lord wants you to do for Him as you serve in your local church in this ministry.

If the Lord has led you to make some specific changes in the way you conduct yourself or in the way you conduct your current ministry, then your goal this week should be to discover what changes need to be made.

Today, list below in the space provided what specific changes the Lord is directing you to make.

What needs to change about *the way I conduct myself*:

Tomorrow, you will continue the process of making these changes to how you conduct yourself as you minister.

If you are unclear or unsure as to what the Lord wants you to do,

Then, surprisingly enough, your goal is the same: to discover what needs you can meet in the local church by serving. However, your initial objective needs to be to discover what it is that the Lord wants you to do to serve Him *while* you are discovering the gifts and talents the Lord has placed within you for serving His people at your local church. It is crucial that you not delay beginning your service in the local church.

It is not necessary for you to understand exactly what or how you will serve in the local church to begin serving the local church. In fact, we learn *how* we are to serve *by* serving. Remember, first we take His yoke upon us, and then we learn (Matthew 11:29).

Today, continue to pray, specifically asking the Lord to show you the needs He wants you to meet and how He wants you to serve in your local church.

Tomorrow, we will continue to discover what specifically the Lord wants you to do for Him, as you serve in your local church.

Journal
Record ideas, impressions, feelings, questions, and any insights you may have had during today's time.

Prayer
Pray for each member of your community.

Conduct in Ministry

DAY TWO

Prayer

Dear Lord, train me to be able to stay focused upon the goals I must reach to accomplish what You have called me to do. Give me the wisdom to discern what is most important from the many matters that urgently present themselves. Help me to do only Your will. Amen.

Core Thought

> Purity of mission means that diffused focus leads to diminished accomplishment.

To minister as Jesus ministered we must come to the belief that there is no more important work to which we are called than ministering in His name. It is the purpose for which we are called and how we are to offer back our lives as a sacrifice of thanksgiving to God (Romans 12:1-2). This ministry is how others experience the love God has for them. It is important that we must not allow ourselves to be distracted by other things, as important as they may seem, from accomplishing what God has declared is, and Jesus has shown to be, the most important mission of all.

When the opportunity to some other good thing presents itself, it is not unusual to become distracted from doing precisely what God has called us to do. Additionally, it is tempting to incorporate additional things into our ministry especially when doing so will enhance it. Several times in Jesus' ministry the opportunity to accomplish additional things other than what directly related to His mission presented itself. It is instructive to see how Jesus dealt with such opportunities:

They [Jesus and the disciples] went to Capernaum, and when the Sabbath came, Jesus went into the synagogue and began to teach. The people were amazed at his teaching, because he taught them as one who had authority, not as the teachers of the law. . . . That evening after sunset the people brought to Jesus all the sick and demon-possessed. The whole town gathered at the door, and Jesus healed many who had various diseases. . . . Very early in the morning, while it was still dark, Jesus got up, left the house and went off to a solitary place, where he prayed. Simon and his companions went to look for him, and when they found him, they exclaimed: "Everyone is looking for you!" Jesus replied, "Let us go somewhere else—to the nearby villages—so I can preach there also. That is why I have come." So he traveled throughout Galilee, preaching in their synagogues and driving out demons (Mark 1:21-22,32-39).

Jesus' ministry was a big hit! People came out in droves to see and hear Him. The disciples thought, "Now we've got something going . . . we're on a roll . . . now they're coming to us!" You can imagine the surprise the disciples felt when the opportunity presented itself for Jesus to stay there and do even more good than the day before and Jesus declined. "But everyone is looking for you . . . what more could you want?" Instead, Jesus directed the focus back to the central focus of His calling, to the purity of His mission, to preach the good news of the kingdom. He reminded them of their mission. They would go on to the next village, "So I can preach there also. That is why I have come."

One afternoon while in a department store I (Bill) walked into the jewelry section and was startled by what I saw. An elderly man stood with his unconscious wife stretched out on the floor in front of him. He was mumbling something like, "I knew we did too much. We were on our feet too long." Obviously, he was entering a mild state of shock. I rushed over and arrived simultaneously with a gaggle of department store personnel. The delegation was armed with chairs, wet cloths, a first-aid kit, and no doubt a legal document or two to be signed. In the midst of the whirling around her, the woman began to regain consciousness. We helped her onto a chair. Someone asked if she needed water. Another asked how she was. An employee questioned, "Do you want anything?" Without any hesitation, the half-awake woman pointed to the jewelry counter. "Yes, I want that silver bracelet." We all burst out laughing, and I thought that there was a woman who never lost sight of her mission.

The Enemy throws many obstacles in the path of obedience, but if our mission is regularly woven into our life, we will remember it just as precisely as the woman in the department store remembered her mission, and we will stick to it even more tenaciously.[1]

Today's Exercises
Core Scripture: 2 Corinthians 5:11-21
Read aloud 2 Corinthians 5:11-21.
Recite this week's memory verse aloud five times.

> Whatever happens, conduct yourselves in a manner worthy of the gospel of Christ. Then, whether I come and see you or only hear about you in my absence, I will know that you stand firm in one spirit, contending as one man for the faith of the gospel. (Philippians 1:27)

Meditate on today's passage.

Request to Be in His Presence
"Dear Lord, bring me into the context of Your world."

1. **Read it**—Remember: We read now only what is there, to hear once again, only what was spoken then. Read 1 Peter 1:17-21 at least twice, out loud.
2. **Think it**—select a portion, a phrase within the reading, and mull it over in your mind, thinking about the context and setting,

---

1. Bill Hull, *Building High Commitment*, 139.

reimagining the event, putting yourself into the situation. As you
meditate, use all five senses to re-create the context and the setting
by building the images that are supplied within the passages.

3. *Pray it*—ask God to give you understanding into how the truths
He has spoken in these Scriptures apply to you now. Ask, "What
is it about me that I need to deal with? What is it about me that
must change?"

   Respond to God by accepting and admitting whatever
responsibility is implied by what He has shown. Write what it is
that God has shown you, and what you must admit responsibility
for having done (or not done).

4. *Live it*—ask God to reveal to you what He wants you to do
about what you have admitted.

State what God has revealed that you must admit responsibility
for doing.

State what particular action(s) you will take today to accomplish
what God has revealed for you to do.

Doing the Discipline

If the Lord has led you to serve in some specific way,

Today,

- Continue to pray, specifically asking the Lord to show you how He wants you to serve within this ministry, how you can meet the needs He wants you to meet.
- List the names and phone numbers of the leaders or contact persons in this ministry.

Leader   Contact   Phone Number

If the Lord has led you to make some specific changes in the way you conduct yourself or in the way you conduct your current ministry, then,

Today list below in the space provided what specific changes the Lord is directing you to make.

What needs to change about the way I conduct my ministry:

If you are unclear or unsure as to what the Lord wants you to do,

Today,

- List in the space provided below the names of three ministries that are currently operating at your local church.

Each should be ministries where it would be possible for you to serve. For example, if you are gifted with the ability to sing or play an instrument you should list "choir," or "praise team," or "worship band." However, if you have contagious tuberculosis you should not list the kitchen or food distribution ministry.

- List the name and phone number of the leader or contact person for each of these ministries.

Leader	Contact	Phone Number

Tomorrow, you will continue the process of making these changes to how you conduct yourself and your ministry.

Journal

Record ideas, impressions, feelings, questions, and any insights you may have had during today's time.

Prayer

Pray for each member of your community.

Conduct in Ministry

DAY THREE

Prayer

Dear Father, help me never to use the people You love, gifts You have given, or the talents You have entrusted to me to advance my own agenda. Please train into the innermost regions of my being the truth that I will only become wholly what I am to be by living my life wholly for You, by living wholly in the service of others and wholly in Jesus' name. Amen.

Core Thought

> Purity of motive means that humble obedience leads to glorious reward but exploitative motives lead to utter disgrace.

We have spoken about what we are to do as ministers and how we are to go about serving others. Today we will discuss the proper motive for ministry. We will discuss the need for us to be rightly motivated in serving others in Jesus' name and the dangers in being otherwise motivated.

The key point to remember about ministry is that when it is done right it benefits everyone involved. So this is a good time to ask the question, "What should it be that motivates us to minister in Jesus' name?" The simple and, by the way, correct answer is love. If this is the correct answer, then why does it seem fuzzy and hard to understand what love in this instance means?

Love ought to be the power that compels us to minister as Jesus ministered. In fact, it is precisely love that was the motivating power that compelled the apostle Paul to minister. "For Christ's love compels us, because we are convinced that one died for all, and therefore all died" (2 Corinthians 5:14). Now the first thing one ought to notice is that it was Christ's love that motivated Paul's actions. This passage's context is about what God has done through Christ to reconcile the world to Himself. Paul is saying that just as the Father's love is in Christ bringing reconciliation to the world, so also is Christ's love at work in us performing the ministry of reconciliation. Therefore, it is Christ's love that motivates Paul to minister, making it possible for him (and us) to continue despite the terrible hardships that he must endure. But what exactly is Christ's love? The short answer is that "Christ's love" is Paul's way of summarizing what Jesus' character allowed Him to do. Christ's character, full of humility, enabled Jesus to submit His will in obedience to His Father's purpose and sacrifice Himself for our sake. "Christ's love" is short for "Jesus' way of loving at work through me." First and foremost, it means humble obedience.

What is clear is that the proper motivation for ministry does not come from our own desires. As we said before, ministry in Jesus' name is something we do for someone else's benefit, without taking into account any benefit to ourselves. This is not something that comes from our natural desires. Rather, our natural desires and way of thinking motivate us in precisely the opposite direction. Our desires naturally compel us to benefit ourselves despite the toll it may take upon others. If we are not compelled by Christ's love in obedience to His commands, then we will naturally act to satisfy our own desires. This can never be ministering in Jesus' name. It will always be self-serving.

We can be very sure of two things. One, when our true motivation for doing ministry is self-satisfaction, we will use the ministry to get what we desire; we will use ministry as a tool for exploitation. Two, exploitative motives lead to exploitive methods; ministry will become an opportunity to sacrifice others to benefit ourselves. The willingness to sacrifice others to benefit oneself is nothing short of blasphemy. It is self-worship, idolatry.

When we are motivated by Christ's love we will serve others *self-sacrificially*. We are motivated by the same kind of love that Jesus shows by humbly obeying His commands, and, like Jesus, our humble obedience now will result in our being extraordinarily exalted in due time (1 Peter 5:4-6).

Today's Exercises
Core Scripture: 2 Corinthians 5:11-21
Read aloud 2 Corinthians 5:11-21.
Recite this week's memory verse aloud five times.

> Whatever happens, conduct yourselves in a manner worthy of the gospel of Christ. Then, whether I come and see you or only hear about you in my absence, I will know that you stand firm in one spirit, contending as one man for the faith of the gospel. (Philippians 1:27)

Meditate on today's passage.

Request to Be in His Presence
"Dear Lord, bring me into the context of Your world."

1. *Read it*—Remember: We read now only what is there, to hear once again, only what was spoken then. Read 1 Peter 1:22-25 at least twice, out loud.
2. *Think it*—select a portion, a phrase within the reading, and mull it over in your mind, thinking about the context and setting, reimagining the event, putting yourself into the situation. As you meditate, use all five senses to re-create the context and the setting by building the images that are supplied within the passages.
3. *Pray it*—ask God to give you understanding into how the truths He has spoken in these Scriptures apply to you now. Ask, "What is it about me that I need to deal with? What is it about me that must change?"

Respond to God by accepting and admitting whatever responsibility is implied by what He has shown. Write what it is that God has shown you, and what you must admit responsibility for having done (or not done).

4. *Live it*—ask God to reveal to you what He wants you to do about what you have admitted.

State what God has revealed that you must admit responsibility for doing.

State what particular action(s) you will take today to accomplish what God has revealed for you to do.

Doing the Discipline

If the Lord has led you to serve in some specific way,

Today,

1. Make appointments to meet (next week, on Day Three, Four, or Five, if possible) individually with each of the current leaders you listed yesterday of the ministry in which the Lord is leading you to serve.
   a. Tell them why you want to meet:
      1. That you are seeking ways that you can serve the Lord in your church, and

    2. That He seems to be leading you to serve in some way that is related to their ministry.

  b. Ask them the three most important or urgent things they would like for you to pray about regarding them or their ministry.

Make a list of their requests.

2. For the next week, present their needs and issues to the Lord. Ask Him if He is leading you to serve to meet these specific needs.

3. Record your appointments below:

	Leader / Contact	Day / Time
1. Day 3		
2. Day 4		
3. Day 5		

If the Lord has led you to make some specific changes in the way you conduct yourself in your current ministry, then,

Today, take the list you made on Day One of this week (containing what needs to change about the way you conduct yourself as you serve in your current ministry) and accomplish these first six steps to begin the process of making the needed changes.

1. Complete the statement below using the first change that you listed (on Day One of this week):

   Lord, I know that I need to change the way *I have been conducting myself as I serve.* What needs to change about me is:

2. Ask the Lord to help you to be honest about what needs to change about the way you conduct yourself and for wisdom to know how to go about making the change.
3. Accept responsibility for any wrongdoing or harm you have caused to others.
4. Write the names of the two people who have suffered the most as a result of the way you have wrongly conducted yourself as you conducted your ministry. Describe how your actions and attitudes have caused them to suffer.

   Person One:

   Person Two:

5. Ask the Lord's forgiveness for having harmed those who have suffered from your conduct, especially for the two you have named above.

If you are unclear or unsure as to what the Lord wants you to do,

Today,
1. Pray, specifically asking the Lord to show you the needs He wants you to meet,
2. Make appointments to meet with each of the three leaders of the ministries you listed yesterday (try to arrange these meetings to take place on Days Three, Four, and Five of Week Four),
   a. Tell them why you want to meet, that you are seeking ways that you can serve the Lord in your church,
   b. Ask them the three most important or urgent things they would like for you to pray about regarding them or their ministry between now and when you meet, and make a list of their requests, and
3. Present their needs and issues to the Lord, asking Him if He is leading you to serve to meet their needs.

Journal
Record ideas, impressions, feelings, questions, and any insights you may have had during today's time.

Prayer
Pray for each member of your community.

Conduct in Ministry

DAY FOUR

Prayer

Dear Lord, train me to enjoy doing what is best. Help me to acquire a taste for doing what You consider to be excellent and for doing excellently what is excellent. Amen.

Core Thought

> Purity of method means that it is not right to do only what is best but that it is best only if it is also done rightly.

Today's culture worships success and adores a successful person. For example, we pay tribute to the achievements of the great barons of business and admire their cunning ways. We seem to be quite willing to blink at or even excuse the cutthroat means and exploitive methods they use to accomplish their objectives. We prize them for building great financial empires and pardon them for laying waste to anyone or thing that lies in their way. Why? Because we continue to fall for the first lie that tempted us and hope that the second lie will be true. The first lie was told to us by another. The second we tell to convince ourselves.

The first lie boiled down to something like this: Doing whatever you can to become the best you can be is always good. The Serpent said it like this: "When you eat of it your eyes will be opened, and you will be like God" (Genesis 3:5). The second lie was that to become the best you can be you must sometimes disobey God. It always sounds something like this: "It was good . . . it is pleasing . . . and it is desirable" (Genesis 3:6).

Desiring to be all we can be and becoming all we can be is exactly what God wants for all of us. His Word is packed with promises of our being made perfect in Christ, of our knowing, seeing, and understanding being made complete, and of our experience of love, justice, honor, thanksgiving, and joy being full. There is indeed nothing sinful in having this desire. He made us so.

God has desired from the beginning that we become all we can be, that we reach our full potential. This is so important to Him that from the beginning He put in place the method by which we are to gain our full potential: humble obedience to His commands and service to others in His name.

So when man first sinned it was not the *desire* to be all we can be that was evil. It was not what we desired or what we intended that was wrong. It was the *way* we chose to accomplish it that was sinful. The method we chose was not the right way to accomplish the right thing. The way we accomplish God's will is part of God's will. We cannot do God's will any other way than His way. *How* ministry is done is just as important as what is done in ministry because ministry is both what is done in service to others and how the service is done for others. In the same way *how* God's will is accomplished is as important as *what* in God's will is being accomplished. Why are the two alike? Because ministering in Jesus' name is exactly this: accomplishing God's will God's way.

To minister as Jesus ministered we will do the right things the right way to best serve others in Jesus' name.

Today's Exercises
Core Scripture: 2 Corinthians 5:11-21
Read aloud 2 Corinthians 5:11-21.
Recite this week's memory verse aloud five times.

Whatever happens, conduct yourselves in a manner worthy of the gospel of Christ. Then, whether I come and see you or only hear about you in my absence, I will know that you stand firm in one spirit, contending as one man for the faith of the gospel. (Philippians 1:27)

Meditate on today's passage.

Request to Be in His Presence

"Dear Lord, bring me into the context of Your world."

1. ***Read it***—Remember: We read now only what is there, to hear once again, only what was spoken then. Read 1 Peter 2:1-6 at least twice, out loud.
2. ***Think it***—select a portion, a phrase within the reading, and mull it over in your mind, thinking about the context and setting, reimagining the event, putting yourself into the situation. As you meditate, use all five senses to re-create the context and the setting by building the images that are supplied within the passages.
3. ***Pray it***—ask God to give you understanding into how the truths He has spoken in these Scriptures apply to you now. Ask, "What is it about me that I need to deal with? What is it about me that must change?"

    Respond to God by accepting and admitting whatever responsibility is implied by what He has shown. Write what it is that God has shown you, and what you must admit responsibility for having done (or not done).
4. ***Live it***—ask God to reveal to you what He wants you to do about what you have admitted.

State what God has revealed that you must admit responsibility for doing.

State what particular action(s) you will take today to accomplish what God has revealed for you to do.

Doing the Discipline

If the Lord has led you to serve in some specific way,

Today,
1. Pray for each of the ministry leaders with whom you will be meeting next week:
   a. About their needs and issues, and
   b. The three most important or urgent things they would like for you to pray about regarding their ministry.
2. Ask the Lord if He is leading you to serve to meet these specific needs.

If the Lord has led you to make some specific changes in the way you conduct yourself in your current ministry, then,

Today, consider the statement you made yesterday regarding the first thing that must change about the way you've been conducting yourself and the two people you named who've been harmed by your conduct, and do the following:

Write below the name of a mature and trustworthy Christian with whom you can discuss these issues. Hopefully, it will be someone in your local church community.

If you are unclear or unsure as to what the Lord wants you to do,

Today, pray for each of the ministry leaders with whom you will be meeting next week:
1. About their needs and issues,
2. The three most important or urgent things they would like for you to pray about regarding their ministry (from Day Three), and
3. If the Lord is leading you to serve to meet these specific needs.

Journal
Record ideas, impressions, feelings, questions, and any insights you may have had during today's time.

Prayer
Pray for each member of your community.

Conduct in Ministry

DAY FIVE

Prayer

Dear Lord, create in me a heart that is completely devoted to bringing You joy and doing whatever is necessary to make Your joy complete. Amen.

Core Thought

> Purity of heart is single-mindedly,
> wholeheartedly loving God by serving others.

When we speak of having purity of heart with regard to ministering in Jesus' name we mean two things: single-mindedness and wholeheartedness. First, purity of heart is shown by single-mindedness in our conduct.

Single-mindedness is the way we will conduct ourselves when integrity of mission is combined with humble obedience. When we serve with single-mindedness our conduct will show that we understand and embrace our calling and intend to accomplish it in whatever way is pleasing to God in obedience to His Word wherever His Spirit leads.

Wholeheartedness is the way we will conduct ourselves when single-mindedness is combined with dynamic devotion. Dynamic devotion occurs when our commitment to accomplishing God's will results in behaviors that are best described as acts of personal sacrifice, acts that in the estimation of most men ought never be considered because they provide no personal gain but which in God's mind are beautiful expressions of worship. When joined with single-mindedness, dynamic acts of devotion show that we understand our calling and the service we give to others is the appropriate sacrifice we are required to offer. Moreover, we delight in doing so. We look for opportunities to minister to others because we develop some of the same tastes that Jesus has. We begin to enjoy serving others because we begin to love them as Jesus loves us. We are being transformed into His image and like Him are becoming filled with grace and truth. The evidence of this transformation will be seen in our behavior.

When those who minister in Jesus' name have purity of heart, single-mindedness, and wholeheartedness, we will see humility, gratefulness, and generosity in the way they conduct the service they have been entrusted with. Look at the purity of heart King David's conduct displays, his single-mindedness and wholeheartedness as he serves his people, before his God:

> So David went down and brought up the ark of God . . . to the City of David with rejoicing. . . . David, wearing a linen ephod, danced before the LORD with all his might, while he and the entire house of Israel brought up the ark of the LORD with shouts and the sound of trumpets. As the ark of the LORD was entering the City of David . . . King David [was] leaping and dancing before the LORD . . . and David sacrificed burnt offerings and fellowship offerings before the LORD. . . . He blessed the people in the name of the LORD Almighty. Then he gave a loaf of bread, a cake of dates and a cake of raisins to each person in the whole crowd of Israelites, both men and women. And all the people went to their homes. . . . Michal daughter of Saul came out to meet him and said, "How the king of Israel has distinguished himself today, disrobing in the sight of the slave girls of his servants as any vulgar fellow would!" David said to Michal, "It was before the LORD, who chose me. . . . I will celebrate before the LORD. I will become even more undignified than this, and I will be humiliated in my own eyes. (2 Samuel 6:12-22)

Having purity of heart means that, like David's, our actions will express our delight in serving our God. We will distinguish ourselves by the extent of our humility, the depth of our devotion, and the generosity of our service. We will be conspicuous because of our lack of self-consciousness as we serve others in Jesus' name.

Today's Exercises

Core Scripture: 2 Corinthians 5:11-21

Read aloud 2 Corinthians 5:11-21.

Recite this week's memory verse aloud five times.

> Whatever happens, conduct yourselves in a manner worthy of the gospel of Christ. Then, whether I come and see you or only hear about you in my absence, I will know that you stand firm in one spirit, contending as one man for the faith of the gospel. (Philippians 1:27)

Meditate on today's passage.

Request to Be in His Presence

"Dear Lord, bring me into the context of Your world."

1. *Read it*—Remember: We read now only what is there, to hear once again, only what was spoken then. Read 1 Peter 2:7-10 at least twice, out loud.
2. *Think it*—select a portion, a phrase within the reading, and mull it over in your mind, thinking about the context and setting, reimagining the event, putting yourself into the situation. As you meditate, use all five senses to re-create the context and the setting by building the images that are supplied within the passages.
3. *Pray it*—ask God to give you understanding into how the truths He has spoken in these Scriptures apply to you now. Ask, "What is it about me that I need to deal with? What is it about me that must change?"

Respond to God by accepting and admitting whatever responsibility is implied by what He has shown. Write what it is that God has shown you, and what you must admit responsibility for having done (or not done).

4. *Live it*—ask God to reveal to you what He wants you to do about what you have admitted.

State what God has revealed that you must admit responsibility for doing.

State what particular action(s) you will take today to accomplish what God has revealed for you to do.

Doing the Discipline
If the Lord has led you to serve in some specific way,

Today,
1. Pray for each of the ministry leaders with whom you will be meeting next week:
   a. About their needs and issues, and
   b. The three most important or urgent things they would like for you to pray about regarding their ministry.
2. Ask the Lord if He is leading you to serve to meet these specific needs.

If the Lord has led you to make some specific changes in the way you conduct yourself in your current ministry, then,

Today, make an appointment to meet (on Day Three, Day Four, or Day Five of Week Five) with the mature and trustworthy Christian you listed yesterday. Explain that you now realize that the way you have conducted yourself as you served others has caused some to experience pain instead of the blessings you had intended. And that you would like to enlist his or her help to accomplish the changes the Lord wants to make in you to be able to minister as Jesus ministered.

Write the day and time of your appointment.

If you are unclear or unsure as to what the Lord wants you to do,

Today, pray for each of the ministry leaders with whom you will be meeting:
1. About their needs and issues,
2. The three most important or urgent things they would like for you to pray about regarding their ministry (From Day Three), and
3. If the Lord is leading you to serve to meet these specific needs.

Journal

Record ideas, impressions, feelings, questions, and any insights you may have had during today's time.

Prayer

Pray for each member of your community.

Conduct in Ministry

DAY SIX

Community Meeting

In preparation for this week's meeting, you will have read and reflected upon each of the week's five Core Thoughts, recorded your thoughts and observations, and are ready to recite this week's memory verse to the group.

WEEK FOUR

Conflict in Ministry

DAY ONE

Prayer

Dear Lord, train me to see conflict as You see it, as grist in the mill of spiritual transformation. Let me respond with grace to those with whom I am engaged in conflict. Let my words be used to bring healing to those who suffer from it. Give me strength to stand firmly in the truth. Amen.

Core Thought

> Ministering in Jesus' name by its very nature is bound to stir up some kind of conflict.

Conflict is produced when differing desires cannot all be fulfilled. Suffering is experienced when someone's desires are not satisfied. Ministering in Jesus' name by its very nature is bound to stir up some kind of conflict.

The purpose of ministering to others is for them to experience God's love in hopes of stirring in them a desire to be reconciled to Him. The fact that there needs to be reconciliation indicates that there is some kind of conflict that needs resolving. One thing we know for sure is that wherever there is conflict we also find suffering. This being the case, it should be no surprise that the conflict that arises from ministering in Jesus' name will be accompanied with suffering by someone somewhere.

The apostle Paul goes so far as to describe this conflict as a war and our ministry as doing warfare (2 Corinthians 10:3-6). History bears witness to the fact that where there is war, there will be those who suffer from it being waged. As ministers of Christ we are not surprised that there is conflict. What often does surprise us is over what the conflict has arisen and who it is that is leading the enemy's assault.

What should be to our shame is that we are almost always shocked when we realize that we are more like our enemies than like Christ's most notable saints. Our desire to have those who oppose us be punished and suffer resembles our Master's desire least and our most notable enemy's most.

To minister as Jesus ministered, we must never shrink from the conflict of the battle nor shy away from suffering for truth. As the battle rages on we must be found serving at our post, binding up the wounds of the faithful with support and encouraging words, praying for strength to endure, loving our enemies, and praying for those who persecute us (Matthew 5:44).

Today's Exercises

Core Scripture: 2 Corinthians 6:12-18

Read aloud 2 Corinthians 6:12-18.

Recite this week's memory verse aloud five times.

> And the God of all grace, who called you to his eternal glory in Christ, after you have suffered a little while, will himself restore you and make you strong, firm and steadfast. (1 Peter 5:10)

Meditate on today's passage.

Request to Be in His Presence

"Dear Lord, bring me into the context of Your world."

1. **Read it**—Remember: We read now only what is there, to hear once again, only what was spoken then. Read 1 Peter 3:8 at least twice, out loud.

2. **Think it**—select a portion, a phrase within the reading, and mull

it over in your mind, thinking about the context and setting, reimagining the event, putting yourself into the situation. As you meditate, use all five senses to re-create the context and the setting by building the images that are supplied within the passages.

3. *Pray it*—ask God to give you understanding into how the truths He has spoken in these Scriptures apply to you now. Ask, "What is it about me that I need to deal with? What is it about me that must change?"

    Respond to God by accepting and admitting whatever responsibility is implied by what He has shown. Write what it is that God has shown you, and what you must admit responsibility for having done (or not done).

4. *Live it*—ask God to reveal to you what He wants you to do about what you have admitted.

State what God has revealed that you must admit responsibility for doing.

State what particular action(s) you will take today to accomplish what God has revealed for you to do.

Doing the Discipline

If the Lord has led you to serve in some specific way,

Today,

1. Pray for each of the ministry leaders with whom you will be meeting this week:
   a. About their needs and issues, and
   b. The three most important or urgent things they would like for you to pray about regarding their ministry;
2. Ask the Lord if He is leading you to serve to meet these specific needs.

If the Lord has led you to make some specific changes in the way you conduct your current ministry, then,

Today, take the list you made on Day Two of Week Three (containing what needs to change about the way you conduct your current ministry) and accomplish these first steps to begin the process of making the needed changes.

1. Complete the statement below using the changes that you listed (on Day Two of Week Three):
   Lord, I know that I need to change the way *I conduct my ministry*. What needs to change about the way I do ministry:

   a.

   b.

c.

2. Pray, asking the Lord to help you to be honest about what needs to change about the way you conduct ministry and for wisdom to know how to go about making the change.
3. List below the first three things that come to mind about your ministry that leads you to believe it is not being conducted the way the Lord desires it to be. Explain how your actions (or inactions) have caused this.

a. I believe I am not conducting ministry the way the Lord desires because . . .

My actions have caused this to be so because I . . .

b. I believe I am not conducting ministry the way the Lord desires because . . .

My actions have caused this to be so because I . . .

c. I believe I am not conducting ministry the way the Lord desires because . . .

My actions have caused this to be so because I . . .

If you are unclear or unsure as to what the Lord wants you to do,

Today, pray for each of the ministry leaders with whom you will be meeting this week:
1. About their needs and issues,
2. The three most important or urgent things they would like for you to pray about regarding their ministry (from Day Three of Week Three), and
3. If the Lord is leading you to serve to meet these specific needs.

Journal

Record ideas, impressions, feelings, questions, and any insights you may have had during today's time.

Prayer

Pray for each member of your community.

Conflict in Ministry

DAY TWO

Prayer

Dear Lord, help me not to compromise when what is true and good
opposes what is false and evil. Train me to prefer suffering for the sake
of what is good rather than desiring any peace that must be purchased
by compromising righteousness. Amen.

Core Thought

> Conflict in ministry occurs when ministers refuse
> to accommodate evil behavior and unsound doctrine.

In an executive management meeting at the company where I (Paul)
worked, the publisher (read "the Big Boss") was voicing his opin-
ions about various matters, punctuating several of them with "Jesus
Christ!" After about the fourth time, the classified advertising manager
(a woman who was respected by no one seated at the table) interrupted
by saying, "I wish you would stop using my Lord's name as a swear
word; it offends me." There followed that unmistakably embarrass-
ing silence that happens when you agree with what was just said but
wish it hadn't been. You feel awkward. "No offense intended," said
the publisher. "It's just an expression. Besides, I think I can speak for
the rest of us in saying that we all believe in some kind of benevolent,
nonintervening deity." While I sat silent, to my surprise the old, vulgar,
press-worn production manager (another person who was not highly
regarded by those present) said, "Speak for yourself" to which there
were nods of agreement from those sitting at the long table. There was

an almost unanimous disagreement with what the Big Boss said. I was amazed at what had come about at that meeting when two people took a stand and opposed what was evil and unsound. I now admired them. They did not see instances where conflict would arise from voicing faith as something that should be avoided. In fact, one commented to me later that they were always amused to see a mocker's face fall when the mocker realized that his audience's silence did not mean that they agreed with him. "They discover what it means to live alone in a house of cards when the wind changes!"

The conflict described above came from the outside. Unfortunately, it is not uncommon for evil behavior and unsound teaching to arise from within the ranks of those who serve in ministries. This brings conflict as well.

We should not be surprised by this. We have been warned of it again and again. The prescription to rid this disease from our ministries is the same as the one necessary to rid the body of anything causing it to be sick. You treat the body, not the sickness. You do whatever is required to restore health to the body. One thing is for certain, ignoring evil and accommodating what is unsound will lead to unhealthy ministry. If evil behavior and unsound doctrine are allowed to live on in any ministry there will be only one sure result, "a sickness unto death" (1 John 5:16).

To minister as Jesus ministered we must not run away from conflict when it presents an opportunity to stand for truth. We must never allow the cancer of evil behavior and unsound doctrine to live untreated among those with whom we minister.

Today's Exercises

Core Scripture: 2 Corinthians 6:12-18
Read aloud 2 Corinthians 6:12-18.
Recite this week's memory verse aloud five times.

> And the God of all grace, who called you to his eternal glory in Christ, after you have suffered a little while, will himself restore you and make you strong, firm and steadfast. (1 Peter 5:10)

Meditate on today's passage.

Request to Be in His Presence
"Dear Lord, bring me into the context of Your world."

1. *Read it*—Remember: We read now only what is there, to hear once again, only what was spoken then. Read 1 Peter 3:9-11 at least twice, out loud.
2. *Think it*—select a portion, a phrase within the reading, and mull it over in your mind, thinking about the context and setting, reimagining the event, putting yourself into the situation. As you meditate, use all five senses to re-create the context and the setting by building the images that are supplied within the passages.
3. *Pray it*—ask God to give you understanding into how the truths He has spoken in these Scriptures apply to you now. Ask, "What is it about me that I need to deal with? What is it about me that must change?"

   Respond to God by accepting and admitting whatever responsibility is implied by what He has shown. Write what it is that God has shown you, and what you must admit responsibility for having done (or not done).
4. *Live it*—ask God to reveal to you what He wants you to do about what you have admitted.

State what God has revealed that you must admit responsibility for doing.

State what particular action(s) you will take today to accomplish what God has revealed for you to do.

Doing the Discipline

If the Lord has led you to serve in some specific way,

Today,

1. Pray for each of the ministry leaders with whom you will be meeting:
   a. About their needs and issues, and
   b. The three most important or urgent things they would like for you to pray about regarding their ministry;
2. Ask the Lord if He is leading you to serve to meet these specific needs.

If the Lord has led you to make some specific changes in the way you conduct your current ministry,

Today, using the list you made on Day Two of last week containing what needs to change about the way you conduct your current ministry, continue the process of making the needed changes and address each of the items.

1. Pray about each issue, asking
   a. For clarity and honesty in your thinking,
   b. That you will be receptive to the Lord's leading as to how each of these issues is to be resolved,
   c. That it will result in your taking the actions necessary to resolve each of these issues, and

      d. That you and those who receive the benefit from your service would begin to experience the full blessings of your obedience, as you continue to minister as Jesus ministered.

2. Journal your progress:
      a. About each issue,
      b. About how your thinking is being changed, and
      c. About the effect of these changes upon your ministry and the people to whom you minister.

3. Share your progress with the members of your community at your weekly community meeting.

If you are unclear or unsure as to what the Lord wants you to do,

Today, pray for each of the ministry leaders with whom you will be meeting this week:

1. About their needs and issues,
2. The three most important or urgent things they would like for you to pray about regarding their ministry (from Day Three of Week Three), and
3. If the Lord is leading you to serve to meet these specific needs.

Journal

Record ideas, impressions, feelings, questions, and any insights you may have had during today's time.

Prayer

Pray for each member of your community.

Conflict in Ministry

DAY THREE

Prayer

Dear Father, teach me to resist being conformed to the world's values. Train me to act in opposition to all that sets itself up against Your will and Your people. Help me never to find comfort by avoiding conflict. Give me the wisdom to know how to confront conflict and honor you. Amen.

Core Thought

> Conflict between culture and ministry arises when truth exposes how people have deviated from doing God's will God's way.

Ministering in Jesus' name will upset the status quo, because it shines the light of God's truth into the cover of darkness under which business as usual is conducted. Conflict between culture and ministry arises when truth exposes how people have deviated from doing God's will God's way. A famous case in point is when Jesus chased the moneychangers from the temple (John 2:12-22). It is an example of what ought to happen when the ways of any culture begin to redefine the mission to which all of God's servants are called.

What is instructive is that there was nothing wrong with the services being provided by the moneychangers. Male Jews were expected to travel to the temple in Jerusalem to celebrate the Passover. They could not very well bring with them the required animals for sacrifice, so a means for purchasing them close to where they would offer them was provided. These were the animals that were driven from the temple. At the same place, they could conveniently pay their annual dues for the support of the temple. Converting the foreign currency of the travelers to the local currency was the service the moneychangers provided. There certainly was nothing wrong with providing these services to the annual worshippers, and Jesus' anger was not directed at this. So what was it that was wrong that Jesus objected to?

Jesus was angry because the very people whom God had chosen to lead all people to Him had become contaminated by their contemporary culture. Instead of drawing all nations to Him they were now leading them away from Him.

The priests were commissioned by God to model for all people how God's servants would minister in the kingdom of God. They were to conduct themselves as chosen servants of the One True God, living according to the rules of His kingdom. The duties they performed in temple worship symbolized the different ways God was bringing redemption to all His people. The temple was built according to a very specific plan, intended to communicate how God has made His presence available to the peoples of all nations. Instead, the priests had succumbed to the culture of their day. They had allowed the get-ahead marketplace mentality of their culture to alter their ministry and to distort the message that the symbol of the temple was meant to communicate.

For the sake of their own personal gain, they moved the services from the marketplace, which had been located outside the temple by the pool of Bethesda (John 5:2) and relocated them inside the temple in the court of the Gentiles. They did this, no doubt, so that they could profit by collecting fees from the merchants for their stands, fees for certifying the sacrificial animals to be without blemish, and collect a percentage of the interest charged for exchanging foreign currency. Make no mistake; it was all about money. The priests were now serving the god Mammon, and they had rededicated the court of the Gentiles to serve his purposes.

What Jesus was angry about was that the servants, the priests that God intended to use to serve His people, were now using His people to serve themselves. They turned the area in the temple that God dedicated to the purpose of bringing the Gentile nations to Himself into a place for merchandising the sale of religious products.

To minister as Jesus ministered His servants must defend His ministry against being distorted and redefined by contemporary culture. To minister in Jesus' name means that His servants will expose the conflict between the values of God's kingdom and the culture of the day with the light of His truth. His servants will overturn and purge the ways of man's culture from the performance of God's ministry.

Today's Exercises

Core Scripture: 2 Corinthians 6:12-18
Read aloud 2 Corinthians 6:12-18.
Recite this week's memory verse aloud five times.

> And the God of all grace, who called you to his eternal glory in Christ, after you have suffered a little while, will himself restore you and make you strong, firm and steadfast. (1 Peter 5:10)

Meditate on today's passage.

Request to Be in His Presence

"Dear Lord, bring me into the context of Your world."

1. **Read it**—Remember: We read now only what is there, to hear once again, only what was spoken then. Read 1 Peter 3:12-13 at least twice, out loud.
2. **Think it**—select a portion, a phrase within the reading, and mull it over in your mind, thinking about the context and setting, reimagining the event, putting yourself into the situation. As you meditate, use all five senses to re-create the context and the setting by building the images that are supplied within the passages.
3. **Pray it**—ask God to give you understanding into how the truths He has spoken in these Scriptures apply to you now. Ask, "What

is it about me that I need to deal with? What is it about me that must change?"

Respond to God by accepting and admitting whatever responsibility is implied by what He has shown. Write what it is that God has shown you, and what you must admit responsibility for having done (or not done).

4. *Live it*—ask God to reveal to you what He wants you to do about what you have admitted.

State what God has revealed that you must admit responsibility for doing.

State what particular action(s) you will take today to accomplish what God has revealed for you to do.

Doing the Discipline

If the Lord has led you to serve in some specific way,

Or,

If you are unclear or unsure as to what the Lord wants you to do,

Today,

1. Pray for each of the ministry leaders with whom you will be meeting this week:

   a. About their needs and issues, and

    b. The three most important or urgent things they would like for you to pray about regarding their ministry;

2. Ask the Lord if He is leading you to serve to meet these specific needs.

If your meeting is scheduled for today,

1. Before you meet, pray:
   a. That your time together would be undisturbed,
   b. That your thinking would be clear,
   c. That you both would be receptive to the Lord's leading, and
   d. That it will result in your knowing what it is that you are to begin doing to minister as Jesus ministered.
   e. About their needs and issues, the three most important or urgent things they would like for you to pray about regarding their ministry (from Day Three of Week Three).
2. Begin your meeting by:
   a. Thanking this leader for taking the time to help you discover how the Lord wants you to serve Him in your local church.
   b. Praying:
      1) That your time together would be undisturbed,
      2) That your thinking would be clear,
      3) That you both would be receptive to the Lord's leading,
      4) That it will result in your knowing what it is that you are to begin doing to minister as Jesus ministered,
      5) About this leader's needs and issues, and
      6) The three most important or urgent things they asked you to pray about regarding their ministry.
3. Continue your meeting by:
   a. Telling the leader that:
      1) You are engaged in a six-week training course which is teaching you how to minister as Jesus ministered, and
      2) You have learned that the process for doing so requires learning how to serve and that is best accomplished by serving (at first) in our own local church,

b. Asking the leader (and noting their answer below):
   1) How their ministry serves the people at your local church?

   2) What led them to become involved in serving in this ministry?

   3) What different ways there are to serve in this ministry?

   4) How you might be used in this ministry?

4. Conclude your meeting by:
   a. Asking the leader:
      1) To pray for you, to ask the Lord to give you guidance during this time of seeking and wisdom to know what to do to best serve Him in your local church, and
      2) To contact you should an appropriate opportunity for you to serve come to their attention,

b. Praying for the leader, asking the Lord to meet their personal needs and the three most important or urgent things they have asked you to pray about regarding their ministry.

If the Lord has led you to make some specific changes in the way you conduct your current ministry,

Today, using the list you made on Day Two of last week containing what needs to change about the way you conduct your current ministry, continue the process of making the needed changes and address each of the items.

1. Pray about each issue, asking
   a. For clarity and honesty in your thinking,
   b. That you will be receptive to the Lord's leading as to how each of these issues is to be resolved,
   c. That it will result in your taking the actions necessary to resolve each of these issues, and
   d. That you and those who receive the benefit from your service would begin to experience the full blessings of your obedience, as you continue to minister as Jesus ministered.
2. Journal your progress:
   a. About each issue,
   b. About how your thinking is being changed, and
   c. About the effect of these changes upon your ministry and the people to whom you minister.
3. Share your progress with the members of your community at your weekly community meeting.

Journal

Record ideas, impressions, feelings, questions, and any insights you may have had during today's time.

Prayer

Pray for each member of your community.

Conflict in Ministry

DAY FOUR

Prayer

Dear Lord, help me not to hold the traditions that have become dear to me with such high regard that I would not be eager to abandon them immediately and gladly if Jesus directed me so. Teach me, Lord, to recognize when traditional or new practices do not honor You or best accomplish Your will. Lord, train me to be eager to abandon my preferences for the sake of serving others in Your name. Amen.

Core Thought

> Conflict between ministry and tradition occurs where the ways for resolving current ministry issues challenge the practicing of a people's long-held traditions.

The conflict arises when ministers refuse to allow a people's long-held traditions to be practiced because they are contrary to God's Word and should be discontinued or when a minister refuses to allow a people's traditions to continue though they are not contrary to God's Word and their practice could be honored.

A great conflict arose in the early years of the Christian church concerning what Gentiles who professed faith in Jesus were required to do to become Christians. On the one side were the Judaizers who insisted that for anyone to become a Christian they must first become one of the people of God. They must in effect become like all true Jews, keepers of the covenant God made with His chosen people, the children of Israel. Because being circumcised was required by the covenant, the Judaizers reasoned that it was still required of those who called Jesus the Messiah. All things considered, this seems quite reasonable except that all things were not being considered. Enter the apostle Paul and with him, conflict.

Paul, considered a very knowledgeable Jew in his day, confronted the Judaizers with the fact that a new covenant had been initiated by God through Christ; the Jews had voided the covenant by their disobedience. (They had, after all, rejected Israel's Messiah, killing Him on a cross!) The old covenant and its practices were no longer in force. There was a new covenant between God and the new Israel, the church. With the new covenant the old practice of physical circumcision was no longer required. The mark that would now distinguish a person as a keeper of the new covenant would be a circumcised heart. The godly actions that are produced by the Spirit of God living out Jesus' life through the believer would be the only outward sign of one's membership. Paul was saying that no one becomes a true believer by first becoming a Jew. One becomes a true Jew by first becoming a believer. Paul insisted that the requirement of circumcision was no longer applicable and that those who were insisting that it continue to be observed were opposed to the clear teaching of God's Word. To insist that anyone continue the practice was to elevate what was now only a tradition from the past above what is and was always true in God's revelation, that we are saved by grace and not by works, that it is a gift of God that cannot be acquired even by doing what is righteous (Ephesians 2:4-14).

As ministers in Christ's service we must not act in preference to the novel simply because it is new, and we must not honor the traditional simply because it has been long held. As with meat, whether it is old or new is not of primary importance. What is paramount is that the meat itself is good. For as the old saying goes, "no matter if meat be old or new, if meat be rotten it will kill you." In these cases, what is most important is that we must not allow our own preferences to decide what is right. Our preferences must fall in submission to the truth of God's Word. Tradition must not trump truth. But where conflict can be resolved without compromising the truth, we must be willing to accommodate the preferences of those we serve.

Conflict occurs when ministers refuse to make accommodations for the preferences and values of those they serve.

Not all things that cause conflict are evil. Sometimes the simple fact that things differ can be the root cause of conflict. This can be seen most often when ministry circumstances bring together peoples with differing cultural values.

When we are sure that neither of the values that are in conflict are evil things, that they are merely different, then ministers must seek to accommodate them wherever possible. Servants who refuse to accommodate the different ways and different manners that may present themselves in ministry are abandoning their position as the Lord's servant and usurping His as Lord over His ministry. As Jesus' servant we have committed ourselves to crucifying our personal preferences to have the freedom to minister to anyone, any way, and anywhere Jesus calls us.

To minister as Jesus ministered, we must resolve conflicts by being gracious in our efforts to accommodate the differences that arise as we minister to those Jesus has called us to serve.

Today's Exercises

Core Scripture: 2 Corinthians 6:12-18

Read aloud 2 Corinthians 6:12-18.

Recite this week's memory verse aloud five times.

> And the God of all grace, who called you to his eternal glory in Christ, after you have suffered a little while, will himself restore you and make you strong, firm and steadfast. (1 Peter 5:10)

Meditate on today's passage.

Request to Be in His Presence

"Dear Lord, bring me into the context of Your world."

1. *Read it*—Remember: We read now only what is there, to hear once again, only what was spoken then. Read 1 Peter 3:14-16 at least twice, out loud.

2. *Think it*—select a portion, a phrase within the reading, and mull it over in your mind, thinking about the context and setting, reimagining the event, putting yourself into the situation. As you meditate, use all five senses to re-create the context and the setting by building the images that are supplied within the passages.

3. *Pray it*—ask God to give you understanding into how the truths He has spoken in these Scriptures apply to you now. Ask, "What is it about me that I need to deal with? What is it about me that must change?"

    Respond to God by accepting and admitting whatever responsibility is implied by what He has shown. Write what it is that God has shown you, and what you must admit responsibility for having done (or not done).

4. *Live it*—ask God to reveal to you what He wants you to do about what you have admitted.

State what God has revealed that you must admit responsibility for doing.

State what particular action(s) you will take today to accomplish what God has revealed for you to do.

Doing the Discipline

If the Lord has led you to serve in some specific way,

Or,

If you are unclear or unsure as to what the Lord wants you to do,

Today,

1. Pray for each of the ministry leaders with whom you will be meeting this week:
   a. About their needs and issues, and
   b. The three most important or urgent things they would like for you to pray about regarding their ministry;
2. Ask the Lord if He is leading you to serve to meet these specific needs.

If your meeting is scheduled for today,

1. Before you meet, pray:
   a. That your time together would be undisturbed,
   b. That your thinking would be clear,
   c. That you both would be receptive to the Lord's leading, and
   d. That it will result in your knowing what it is that you are to begin doing to minister as Jesus ministered.
   e. About their needs and issues, the three most important or urgent things they would like for you to pray about regarding their ministry (from Day Three of Week Three).
2. Begin your meeting by:
   a. Thanking this leader for taking the time to help you discover how the Lord wants you to serve Him in your local church.
   b. Praying:
      1) That your time together would be undisturbed,
      2) That your thinking would be clear,
      3) That you both would be receptive to the Lord's leading,
      4) That it will result in your knowing what it is that you are to begin doing to minister as Jesus ministered,

       5) About this leader's needs and issues, and

       6) The three most important or urgent things they asked you to pray about regarding their ministry.

3. Continue your meeting by:

  a. Telling the leader that:

      1) You are engaged in a six-week training course which is teaching you how to minister as Jesus ministered, and

      2) You have learned that the process for doing so requires learning how to serve and that is best accomplished by serving (at first) in our own local church,

  b. Asking the leader (and noting their answer below):

      1) How their ministry serves the people at your local church?

      2) What led them to become involved in serving in this ministry?

      3) What different ways there are to serve in this ministry?

      4) How you might be used in this ministry?

4. Conclude your meeting by:
   a. Asking the leader:
      1) To pray for you, to ask the Lord to give you guidance during this time of seeking and wisdom to know what to do to best serve Him in your local church, and
      2) To contact you should an appropriate opportunity for you to serve come to their attention,
   b. Praying for the leader, asking the Lord to meet their personal needs and the three most important or urgent things they have asked you to pray about regarding their ministry.

If the Lord has led you to make some specific changes in the way you conduct your current ministry,

Today, using the list you made on Day Two of last week containing what needs to change about the way you conduct your current ministry, continue the process of making the needed changes and address each of the items.

1. Pray about each issue, asking
   a. For clarity and honesty in your thinking,
   b. That you will be receptive to the Lord's leading as to how each of these issues is to be resolved,
   c. That it will result in your taking the actions necessary to resolve each of these issues, and
   d. That you and those who receive the benefit from your service would begin to experience the full blessings of your obedience, as you continue to minister as Jesus ministered.
. Journal your progress:
   a. About each issue,
   b. About how your thinking is being changed, and
   c. About the effect of these changes upon your ministry and the people to whom you minister.
3. Share your progress with the members of your community at your weekly community meeting.

Journal

Record ideas, impressions, feelings, questions, and any insights you may have had during today's time.

Prayer

Pray for each member of your community.

Conflict in Ministry

DAY FIVE

Prayer

Dear Lord, teach me to see conflict as a tool for refining my character. Train me, Lord, to respond in conflict with a willingness to suffer for standing for the truth and opposing what is evil. Amen.

Core Thought

> Conflict results in peace when suffering is the product of doing good.

A terrible mistake is to think that all conflict is a bad thing. A worse mistake is to desire immediate peace so fervently that we compromise what we know is right and good to preserve it. How many relationships continue on in dysfunction because no one is willing to endure the pain of conflict to bring about the changes necessary to resolve the issues and thereby have true peace? But conflict and Jesus' command that we be peace seekers and peacemakers are not incompatible.

Conflict, as we learned early about temptation, is a tool God uses to bring about transformation. Conflict when engaged in properly provides the opportunity for change to occur. Conflict forces us to consider the difference between what is and what ought to be. We see conflict presented this way in Jesus saying:

> Do not suppose that I have come to bring peace to the earth. I did not come to bring peace, but a sword. For I have come to turn "a man against his father, a daughter against her mother,

a daughter-in-law against her mother-in-law—a man's enemies will be the members of his own household." Anyone who loves his father or mother more than me is not worthy of me; anyone who loves his son or daughter more than me is not worthy of me; and anyone who does not take his cross and follow me is not worthy of me. Whoever finds his life will lose it, and whoever loses his life for my sake will find it. (Matthew 10:34-39)

Clearly Jesus is teaching that the suffering that comes as a result of being obedient to our calling as His disciples and honoring His command for us to serve those He seeks to redeem is the cost that we must pay to minister as He ministered.

Conflict does not cause peace, but true peace is rarely sought until we are forced to realize the extent of suffering that we must endure to have what we desire. Conflict provides the occasions for us to consider what we truly want and understand the price that must be paid to have it. It is in conflict that we prove our commitment to what we value by the extent of our sacrificing for it.

To minister as Jesus ministered is to consider the suffering that we must endure while we are obeying the Lord's will and serving in His name as the way we offer ourselves, our lives, to Him as a living sacrifice. It is a reasonable cost to pay for the privilege of serving Him.

Today's Exercises

Core Scripture: 2 Corinthians 6:12-18

Read aloud 2 Corinthians 6:12-18.

Recite this week's memory verse aloud five times.

And the God of all grace, who called you to his eternal glory in Christ, after you have suffered a little while, will himself restore you and make you strong, firm and steadfast. (1 Peter 5:10)

Meditate on today's passage.

Request to Be in His Presence

"Dear Lord, bring me into the context of Your world."

1. *Read it*—Remember: We read now only what is there, to hear once again, only what was spoken then. Read 1 Peter 3:17-22 at least twice, out loud.
2. *Think it*—select a portion, a phrase within the reading, and mull it over in your mind, thinking about the context and setting, reimagining the event, putting yourself into the situation. As you meditate, use all five senses to re-create the context and the setting by building the images that are supplied within the passages.
3. *Pray it*—ask God to give you understanding into how the truths He has spoken in these Scriptures apply to you now. Ask, "What is it about me that I need to deal with? What is it about me that must change?"

   Respond to God by accepting and admitting whatever responsibility is implied by what He has shown. Write what it is that God has shown you, and what you must admit responsibility for having done (or not done).
4. *Live it*—ask God to reveal to you what He wants you to do about what you have admitted.

State what God has revealed that you must admit responsibility for doing.

State what particular action(s) you will take today to accomplish what God has revealed for you to do.

Doing the Discipline

If the Lord has led you to serve in some specific way,

Or,

If you are unclear or unsure as to what the Lord wants you to do,

Today,

1. Pray for each of the ministry leaders with whom you will be meeting this week:
   a. About their needs and issues, and
   b. The three most important or urgent things they would like for you to pray about regarding their ministry;
2. Ask the Lord if He is leading you to serve to meet these specific needs.

If your meeting is scheduled for today,

1. Before you meet, pray:
   a. That your time together would be undisturbed,
   b. That your thinking would be clear,
   c. That you both would be receptive to the Lord's leading, and
   d. That it will result in your knowing what it is that you are to begin doing to minister as Jesus ministered.
   e. About their needs and issues, the three most important or urgent things they would like for you to pray about regarding their ministry (from Day Three of Week Three),
2. Begin your meeting by:

    a. Thanking this leader for taking the time to help you discover how the Lord wants you to serve Him in your local church.

    b. Praying:

       1) That your time together would be undisturbed,

       2) That your thinking would be clear,

       3) That you both would be receptive to the Lord's leading,

       4) That it will result in your knowing what it is that you are to begin doing to minister as Jesus ministered,

       5) About this leader's needs and issues, and

       6) The three most important or urgent things they asked you to pray about regarding their ministry.

3. Continue your meeting by:

    a. Telling the leader that:

       1) You are engaged in a six-week training course which is teaching you how to minister as Jesus ministered, and

       2) You have learned that the process for doing so requires learning how to serve and that is best accomplished by serving (at first) in our own local church,

    b. Asking the leader (and noting their answer below):

       1) How their ministry serves the people at your local church?

       2) What led them to become involved in serving in this ministry?

       3) What different ways there are to serve in this ministry?

       4) how you might be used in this ministry?

  4. Conclude your meeting by:
     a. Asking the leader:
       1) To pray for you, to ask the Lord to give you guidance during this time of seeking and wisdom to know what to do to best serve Him in your local church, and
       2) To contact you should an appropriate opportunity for you to serve come to their attention,
     b. Praying for the leader, asking the Lord to meet their personal needs and the three most important or urgent things they have asked you to pray about regarding their ministry.

If the Lord has led you to make some specific changes in the way you conduct your current ministry,

Today, using the list you made on Day Two of last week containing what needs to change about the way you conduct your current ministry, continue the process of making the needed changes and address each of the items.

  1. Pray about each issue, asking
     a. For clarity and honesty in your thinking,
     b. That you will be receptive to the Lord's leading as to how each of these issues is to be resolved,
     c. That it will result in you taking the actions necessary to resolve each of these issues, and
     d. That you and those who receive the benefit from your service would begin to experience the full blessings of your obedience, as you continue to minister as Jesus ministered.
  2. Journal your progress:

   a. About each issue,

   b. About how your thinking is being changed, and

   c. About the effect of these changes upon your ministry and the people to whom you minister.

3. Share your progress with the members of your community at your weekly community meeting.

Journal

Record ideas, impressions, feelings, questions, and any insights you may have had during today's time.

Prayer

Pray for each member of your community.

Conflict in Ministry

DAY SIX

Community Meeting

In preparation for this week's meeting, you will have read and reflected upon each of the week's five Core Thoughts, recorded your thoughts and observations, and are ready to recite this week's memory verse to the group.

WEEK FIVE

Capacity for Ministry

DAY ONE

Prayer

Dear Lord, help me to place myself in the care of Your people, to trust myself to Your care in their hands. Teach me to minister as Jesus ministered. Help me learn how to minister by witnessing how You continually give of Yourself through the service of Your children. Amen.

Core Thought

> Living in community is how we experience God's capacity to minister to us through the service of others.

Living in community with other believers is how we become aware of the central part that ministering to others plays in our own spiritual formation and in the advancement of God's kingdom. The normal way we experience the love God has for us is through the people within whose midst He has placed us. It is also within the community of believers that we learn how to minister as Jesus ministered. God intends for us to receive His love through the community of His people. We are told specifically that where two or more of His servants are gathered in His name He will be in their midst (Matthew 18:20). Living in community with other believers and serving them provides the personal interaction and the relational traction that the Holy Spirit uses to transform us and the service we give to others.

Because the very nature of ministry in Jesus' name is serving others and learning to do so can only be accomplished by actually serving others, it is impossible to learn to minister as Jesus ministered in isolation. Of course, the Lord has provided the perfect training venues for ministry: first, at home with family, and second, in community with other believers (usually within a local church).

At home we learn what caring for others is and how to do it by being cared for by others. Likewise, within the community of believers we learn to serve others by experiencing our needs being met by God through others.

The home and local church can be so effective at preparing and training believers to carry on Jesus' ministry that it is no surprise that the Devil should concentrate a great deal of effort toward their destruction. And the Devil's most successful tactic for disrupting Jesus' ministry is to separate a believer from the very thing that will prepare and train him for servant ministry: living in community with other believers. If a believer is isolated from those who comprise his local family of believers, then the Devil, like a prowling lion, can devour him, and he will never bless nor receive the blessings that come from ministering in Jesus' name.

Today's Exercises

Core Scripture: 2 Corinthians 6:1-11
Read aloud 2 Corinthians 6:1-11.
Recite this week's memory verse aloud five times.

> Each one should use whatever gift he has received to serve others, faithfully administering God's grace in its various forms.
> (1 Peter 4:10)

Meditate on today's passage.

Request to Be in His Presence
"Dear Lord, bring me into the context of Your world."

1. *Read it*—Remember: We read now only what is there, to hear once again, only what was spoken then. Read 1 Peter 2:1-12 at least twice, out loud.

2. *Think it*—select a portion, a phrase within the reading, and mull it over in your mind, thinking about the context and setting, reimagining the event, putting yourself into the situation. As you meditate, use all five senses to re-create the context and the setting by building the images that are supplied within the passages.

3. *Pray it*—ask God to give you understanding into how the truths He has spoken in these Scriptures apply to you now. Ask, "What is it about me that I need to deal with? What is it about me that must change?"

   Respond to God by accepting and admitting whatever responsibility is implied by what He has shown. Write what it is that God has shown you, and what you must admit responsibility for having done (or not done).

4. *Live it*—ask God to reveal to you what He wants you to do about what you have admitted.

State what God has revealed that you must admit responsibility for doing.

State what particular action(s) you will take today to accomplish what God has revealed for you to do.

Doing the Discipline

If you are unclear or unsure as to what the Lord wants you to do,

From the beginning we said that your goal was to discover what needs you can meet in the local church by serving and that your initial objective was to discover what it is that the Lord wants you to do to serve Him *while* you are discovering the gifts and talents the Lord has placed within you for serving His people at your local church. Also, it is crucial that you not delay beginning your service in the local church because you will learn how to serve by serving.

Today, you will begin ministering in Jesus' name by selecting a particular local church ministry in which to serve.

Based upon what you've learned and upon any leading by the Lord you may be sensing about each of the ministries into which you have enquired, take the following steps.

1. Select one ministry from among the three you listed and met about.
   a. Call the leader of that ministry and tell him that you would like to begin serving in their ministry.
   b. Ask him to consider using you and your abilities to meet whatever needs are lacking in their ministry,
2. Make a commitment to the Lord, this leader, and the others who serve in this ministry to faithfully serve for the next seven weeks.
3. Begin serving in this ministry as soon as possible. Know what you are expected to do, when, and with whom.
4. Include your experiences in your daily journaling.
5. Share your experience with the members of your community at the weekly community meeting.

Journal

Record ideas, impressions, feelings, questions, and any insights you may have had during today's time.

Prayer

Pray for each member of your community.

Capacity for Ministry

DAY TWO

Prayer

Dear Lord, make me aware of the many ways Your love is being presented to others by the service Your people do in Your name. Open my mind to recognize whatever it is that You are calling me to do in Your name. Amen.

Core Thought

> Training in community is how God
> prepared in us the capacity to minister.

Living in community makes us aware of God's love as we experience it through another believer's capacity to minister to us. Through training within a community of believers God prepares in us the capacity to minister.

Capacity can be thought of as a container for holding all that is necessary for us to provide the same excellence of service to others that Jesus gave. Within this container we will find such things as awareness, intention, knowledge, skills, and perseverance.

We first become aware of ministry and begin to understand that we have a part to play in Jesus' ministry by receiving God's blessings through the service of others. This usually occurs at home with our family and at our local church. Through the various interactions we have with others, God begins to train within us the intention to move from being someone who merely enjoys being served by others to becoming someone who will be a joyful servant of others. This training is intended to be provided to believers by servants whom Jesus has specially gifted for the purpose of equipping believers to do the work of the ministry (Ephesians 4:11-13).

Under the teachers that Jesus has called to minister within the local church our intentions mature into understanding our own calling to ministry. We learn the "what" of ministry.

Through gifted pastors and teachers we learn *what* ministry in Jesus' name is. By interacting with others who are discovering their calling and their gifting and by serving them, we can begin to see what the Lord is calling us to do.

Serving other believers and serving with other believers will reveal the gifting you have been given. Your gifting and the direction of your calling will most often be confirmed and affirmed by those who have experienced your ministering (2 Timothy 1:3-6).

Today's Exercises

Core Scripture: 2 Corinthians 6:1-11
Read aloud 2 Corinthians 6:1-11.
Recite this week's memory verse aloud five times.

> Each one should use whatever gift he has received to serve others, faithfully administering God's grace in its various forms. (1 Peter 4:10)

Meditate on today's passage.

Request to Be in His Presence

"Dear Lord, bring me into the context of Your world."

1. **Read it**—Remember: We read now only what is there, to hear once again, only what was spoken then. Read 1 Peter 2:13-15 at least twice, out loud.
2. **Think it**—select a portion, a phrase within the reading, and mull it over in your mind, thinking about the context and setting, reimagining the event, putting yourself into the situation. As you

meditate, use all five senses to re-create the context and the setting by building the images that are supplied within the passages.

3. *Pray it*—ask God to give you understanding into how the truths He has spoken in these Scriptures apply to you now. Ask, "What is it about me that I need to deal with? What is it about me that must change?"

   Respond to God by accepting and admitting whatever responsibility is implied by what He has shown. Write what it is that God has shown you, and what you must admit responsibility for having done (or not done).

4. *Live it*—ask God to reveal to you what He wants you to do about what you have admitted.

State what God has revealed that you must admit responsibility for doing.

State what particular action(s) you will take today to accomplish what God has revealed for you to do.

Doing the Discipline

If the Lord has led you to serve in some specific way,

Today,

1. Pray for each of the ministry leaders with whom you will be meeting:

a. About their needs and issues, and

b. The three most important or urgent things they would like for you to pray about regarding their ministry;

2. Ask the Lord if He is leading you to serve to meet these specific needs.

If the Lord has led you to make some specific changes in the way you conduct your current ministry,

Today, using the list you made on Day Two of last week containing what needs to change about the way you conduct your current ministry, continue the process of making the needed changes and address each of the items.

1. Pray about each issue, asking

a. For clarity and honesty in your thinking,

b. That you will be receptive to the Lord's leading as to how each of these issues is to be resolved,

c. That it will result in you taking the actions necessary to resolve each of these issues, and

d. That you and those who receive the benefit from your service would begin to experience the full blessings of your obedience, as you continue to minister as Jesus ministered.

2. Journal your progress:

a. About each issue,

b. About how your thinking is being changed, and

c. About the effect of these changes upon your ministry and the people to whom you minister.

3. Share your progress with the members of your community at your weekly community meeting.

If you are unclear or unsure as to what the Lord wants you to do,

Today, pray for each of the ministry leaders with whom you will be meeting:

1. About their needs and issues,
2. The three most important or urgent things they would like for you to pray about regarding their ministry, and
3. If the Lord is leading you to serve to meet these specific needs.

If your meeting is scheduled for today,

1. Before you meet, pray:
   a. That your time together would be undisturbed,
   b. That your thinking would be clear,
   c. That you both would be receptive to the Lord's leading, and
   d. That it will result in your knowing what it is that you are to begin doing to minister as Jesus ministered.
2. Begin your meeting by:
   a. Thanking this leader for taking the time to help you discover how the Lord wants you to serve Him in your local church.
   b. Praying:
      1) That your time together would be undisturbed,
      2) That your thinking would be clear,
      3) That you both would be receptive to the Lord's leading,
      4) That it will result in your knowing what it is that you are to begin doing to minister as Jesus ministered,
      5) About this leader's needs and issues, and
      6) The three most important or urgent things they asked you to pray about regarding their ministry.
3. Continue your meeting by:
   a. Telling the leader that:
      1) You are engaged in a six-week training course which is teaching you how to minister as Jesus ministered, and
      2) You have learned that the process for doing so requires learning how to serve and that is best accomplished by serving (at first) in our own local church,
   b. Asking the leader (and noting their answer below):
      1) How their ministry serves the people at your local church

2) What led them to become involved in serving in this ministry

3) What different ways there are to serve in this ministry

4) How you might be used in this ministry

4. Conclude your meeting by:
   a. Asking the leader:
      1) To pray for you, asking the Lord to give you guidance during this time of seeking and wisdom to know what to do to best serve Him in your local church, and
      2) To contact you should an appropriate opportunity for you to serve come to their attention,
   b. Praying for the leader, asking the Lord to meet their personal needs and the three most important or urgent things they have asked you to pray about regarding their ministry.

Journal

Record ideas, impressions, feelings, questions, and any insights you may have had during today's time.

Prayer

Pray for each member of your community.

Capacity for Ministry

DAY THREE

Prayer

Dear Father, give me boldness today to step out and begin to serve You with a clear sense of purpose. I place my trust in Your abundance to supply me with whatever I lack, and I look for the opportunities to serve You that You have placed in my path, knowing that through them You intend to bless me. Amen.

Core Thought

Serving in community is how God strengthens our capacity to minister.

The training we receive under gifted pastors equips us to serve others by growing in us an awareness about ministry and the intention to serve. Gifted teachers grow in us an understanding of what ministering in Jesus' name is, its purpose, the various forms ministry can take, and how we can discover our gifting and individual calling. Pastors and teachers often make us aware of ministry opportunities and particular needs that arise within a community of believers. Often through these opportunities to serve we will discover our gifting, and our calling is confirmed. It is when we commit to fulfilling the need offered by these opportunities that we begin the most exciting and transforming aspect of ministry.

Nothing is more exciting than experiencing God working through You to accomplish His will, and, there is no better means for deep and lasting spiritual growth than through serving Christ under godly leaders. This means allowing all aspects of your ministering (what you do, how you do it, and for whom you do it) to be reviewed and evaluated by people who are known for their faithful service to Christ. When we perform our service under the watchful eyes of godly servants, we are held accountable for keeping our commitments to God, we are encouraged to exercise our gifts, our areas of strength are affirmed, and our ability to minister is protected from being compromised by our areas of weakness and by deficiencies in our character, conduct, and skill set.

Whatever gifts we possess came from the Holy Spirit and do not belong to us. The Holy Spirit's power was placed in our capacity. It is not an enhancement of something that was there previously. His gifting is not an upgrade. It is the gift of His power working though us. The gift was given to us with the intention that we would learn how to correctly dispense it to benefit the church. When we do so, we are serving the church. It makes sense then that God would provide specially gifted leaders to train us in how best to dispense His power to serve His people.

Today's Exercises
Core Scripture: 2 Corinthians 6:1-11
Read aloud 2 Corinthians 6:1-11.
Recite this week's memory verse aloud five times.

> Each one should use whatever gift he has received to serve others, faithfully administering God's grace in its various forms. (1 Peter 4:10)

Meditate on today's passage.

Request to Be in His Presence
"Dear Lord, bring me into the context of Your world."

1. **Read it**—Remember: We read now only what is there, to hear once again, only what was spoken then. Read 1 Peter 2:16-20 at least twice, out loud.

2. ***Think it***—select a portion, a phrase within the reading, and mull it over in your mind, thinking about the context and setting, reimagining the event, putting yourself into the situation. As you meditate, use all five senses to re-create the context and the setting by building the images that are supplied within the passages.

3. ***Pray it***—ask God to give you understanding into how the truths He has spoken in these Scriptures apply to you now. Ask, "What is it about me that I need to deal with? What is it about me that must change?"

    Respond to God by accepting and admitting whatever responsibility is implied by what He has shown. Write what it is that God has shown you, and what you must admit responsibility for having done (or not done).

4. ***Live it***—ask God to reveal to you what He wants you to do about what you have admitted.

State what God has revealed that you must admit responsibility for doing.

State what particular action(s) you will take today to accomplish what God has revealed for you to do.

Today, make an appointment to meet (on Day Three, Day Four, or Day Five of Week Five) with the mature and trustworthy Christian you listed yesterday. Explain that you now realize that the way you have conducted yourself as you served others has caused some to experience pain instead of the blessings you had intended. And that you would like to enlist their help to accomplish the changes the Lord wants to make in you to be able to minister as Jesus ministered.

Doing the Discipline

If the Lord has led you to make some specific changes in the way you conduct yourself in your current ministry, and your meeting with a mature and trustworthy Christian is scheduled for today, then,

1. Before you meet, pray:
    a. That your time together would be undisturbed,
    b. That your thinking would be clear,
    c. That you both would be receptive to the Lord's leading, and
    d. That it will result in your knowing what in particular you are to begin doing to partner with the Holy Spirit to transform the way *you conduct yourself* to enable you to minister as Jesus ministered.
2. Begin your meeting by:
    a. Thanking this person for taking the time to help you discover how to better serve the Lord by better conducting yourself as you minister to His people in your local church.
    b. Praying:
        1) That your time together would be undisturbed,
        2) That your thinking would be clear,
        3) That you both would be receptive to the Lord's leading,
        4) That it will result in your knowing what it is that you are to begin doing to minister as Jesus ministered.
3. Continue your meeting by:
    a. Telling them that:
        1) You are engaged in a six-week training course which is teaching you how to minister as Jesus ministered, and
        2) You have learned that the process for doing so requires learning how to serve, and that this is best accomplished by

serving the people in our own local church,

3) You have been praying and fasting with the intention that the Lord would bring to your mind anything regarding how you conduct yourself as you minister to others which may be keeping them from receiving the blessings the Lord wants to give them through you.

4) You have identified changes that must be made,

5) You have identified people who were damaged by your misconduct, have confessed and repented,

6) You would like their help to make the necessary changes in the way you conduct yourself as you minister.

b. Sharing with them, using the lists and responses you made Doing the Disciplines in Weeks Two, Three, and Four:

1) What the Lord has been revealing to you about your conduct in ministry,

c. Asking with them to offer any questions, comments, insights, and wise counsel they have for you to consider.

4. Conclude your meeting by:

a. Asking this person:

1) To pray for you, asking the Lord to give you during this time of seeking and wisdom to know what to do to best serve Him in your local church, and

2) To speak into your life, and hold you accountable for keeping the commitments you have made to the Lord to change how you conduct yourself when ministering,

b. Praying for this person, asking the Lord to meet their personal needs, bless their time with Him, and thanking the Lord for making Himself available to you through this person.

Journal

Record ideas, impressions, feelings, questions, and any insights
you may have had during today's time.

Prayer

Pray for each member of your community.

Capacity for Ministry

DAY FOUR

Prayer

Dear Lord, train me to remain flexible and moldable as You continue to conform me to the image of Your Son. Use the difficulties and challenges that I will face today as I serve Your people to transform me into a servant with the capacity to minister as Jesus ministered. Amen.

Core Thought

> Adapting to changes in our community
> is how God extends our capacity to minister.

"Nobody likes change," we are told, but what people really don't like is changing something that is satisfying to them, something that they believe works for them. The real reason people don't like change is that they fear losing that satisfaction to which they have become accustomed. So the instant someone talks about making changes you see a worried look on the faces of those whom the changes will affect. We must admit that oftentimes we all share this fear. However all Christians are called to minister in Jesus' name, and when we are obedient to this calling, our service to others makes a difference. It brings about change into the lives of the people it touches. For us to fulfill our calling to Christ, we must help those we serve adapt to the changes that our ministering brings their way. To do this, we must become someone who no longer views change with fear but recognizes change as an opportunity to exercise our ability to adapt our ministering to the changes that affect where we live, work, and play. The place that God has designed to initiate this training is in the company of committed believers in the local church.

Anyone who has spent more than a brief time with a group of committed believers knows that the dynamic interchange of ideas, life events, interpersonal conflicts, and ministry challenges causes change to abound. The local church has a lot going on and a lot of changing going on. This makes it the perfect training ground for learning how to extend our ministry by causing us to adapt to changes in the community of believers.

A healthy, committed group of believers provides the kind of environment necessary for nurturing the skill of adapting to change. Adapting is crucial for bringing change into the lives of those to whom we minister, and developing this skill is crucial if we are to extend our ministry to those who are not yet members of the household of faith.

Today's Exercises
Core Scripture: 2 Corinthians 6:1-11
Read aloud 2 Corinthians 6:1-11.
Recite this week's memory verse aloud five times.

> Each one should use whatever gift he has received to serve others, faithfully administering God's grace in its various forms. (1 Peter 4:10)

Meditate on today's passage.

Request to Be in His Presence
"Dear Lord, bring me into the context of Your world."

1. **Read it**—Remember: We read now only what is there, to hear once again, only what was spoken then. Read 1 Peter 2:21-25 at least twice, out loud.
2. **Think it**—select a portion, a phrase within the reading, and mull it over in your mind, thinking about the context and setting,

reimagining the event, putting yourself into the situation. As you meditate, use all five senses to re-create the context and the setting by building the images that are supplied within the passages.

3. ***Pray it***—ask God to give you understanding into how the truths He has spoken in these Scriptures apply to you now. Ask, "What is it about me that I need to deal with? What is it about me that must change?"

    Respond to God by accepting and admitting whatever responsibility is implied by what He has shown. Write what it is that God has shown you, and what you must admit responsibility for having done (or not done).

4. ***Live it***—ask God to reveal to you what He wants you to do about what you have admitted.

State what God has revealed that you must admit responsibility for doing.

State what particular action(s) you will take today to accomplish what God has revealed for you to do.

Doing the Discipline

If the Lord has led you to make some specific changes in the way you conduct yourself in your current ministry, and your meeting with a mature and trustworthy Christian is scheduled for today, then,

Perform the steps in Day Three.

Journal

Record ideas, impressions, feelings, questions, and any insights you may have had during today's time.

Prayer

Pray for each member of your community.

Capacity for Ministry

DAY FIVE

Prayer
Dear Lord, thank You for placing me within a community of believers for my safety and growth and as a sure way to enjoy Your blessings. Amen.

Core Thought

> Celebrating in community is how
> God revives our capacity to minister.

To minister as Jesus ministered, we must not only be fully equipped to perform the services to others. We must be fully available to respond to Jesus when He calls upon us to serve others. Yes, we must be part of a community that makes us aware of our need to serve and prepares and trains us to minister to others. Yes, we must allow our brothers and sisters to provide us with the critical and constructive feedback we need to improve our skills and expand our capacity to minister. Each and all of these are essential, but they are not enough to give us the same capacity to minister as Jesus had. They train in us the ability to minister, but they do not grow in us the availability to minister.

The availability to minister is simply the wholehearted desire to serve others as an offering of thanksgiving to God in appreciation for the love He has shown to us. This desire to offer our service as a sacrifice of thanksgiving to God must be tended like embers in a fire. It must be nourished with fresh dry fuel and fanned into flame for it to do its work. If it is not attended by the keeper of the flame and continues to do its work unstoked by its keeper, its light will dim, its heat will cool, and only the charred remains will survive where once a warm, lively, and attractive fire was enjoyed by all whose path crossed its way.

To minister as Jesus ministered we must remain available to minister. We do this by celebrating our thankfulness to God with other believers. We put away our usual work and reserve special times to celebrate how wonderful the God we love is and to recount the wonderful things He has done. This is worship. We dedicate this time to recognize God's greatness and His goodness, and we use this as the appropriate time for reaffirming our commitment to serve Him. During this time of worship we offer ourselves in service to others as a living sacrifice of thanksgiving to Him. In doing so, the Holy Spirit (the keeper of the fire) stokes the embers that live within us, fanning them into flames, reviving our desire to wholeheartedly serve Him. Celebrating God in the community of believers makes our capacity to minister available for God's use by reviving our desire to minister in Jesus' name.

Today's Exercises
Core Scripture: 2 Corinthians 6:1-11
Read aloud 2 Corinthians 6:1-11.
Recite this week's memory verse aloud five times.

> Each one should use whatever gift he has received to serve others, faithfully administering God's grace in its various forms. (1 Peter 4:10)

Meditate on today's passage.

Request to Be in His Presence
"Dear Lord, bring me into the context of Your world."

1. *Read it*—Remember: We read now only what is there, to hear once again, only what was spoken then. Read 1 Peter 3:7 at least twice, out loud.

2. ***Think it***—select a portion, a phrase within the reading, and mull it over in your mind, thinking about the context and setting, reimagining the event, putting yourself into the situation. As you meditate, use all five senses to re-create the context and the setting by building the images that are supplied within the passages.

3. ***Pray it***—ask God to give you understanding into how the truths He has spoken in these Scriptures apply to you now. Ask, "What is it about me that I need to deal with? What is it about me that must change?"

   Respond to God by accepting and admitting whatever responsibility is implied by what He has shown. Write what it is that God has shown you, and what you must admit responsibility for having done (or not done).

4. ***Live it***—ask God to reveal to you what He wants you to do about what you have admitted.

   State what God has revealed that you must admit responsibility for doing.

   State what particular action(s) you will take today to accomplish what God has revealed for you to do.

Doing the Discipline

If the Lord has led you to make some specific changes in the way you
conduct yourself in your current ministry, and your meeting with a
mature and trustworthy Christian is scheduled for today, then,

Perform the steps in Day Three.

Journal

Record ideas, impressions, feelings, questions, and any insights
you may have had during today's time.

Prayer

Pray for each member of your community.

Capacity for Ministry

DAY SIX

Community Meeting

In preparation for this week's meeting, you will have read and reflected upon each of the week's five Core Thoughts, recorded your thoughts and observations, and are ready to recite this week's memory verse to the group.

WEEK SIX

Compassion in Ministry

DAY ONE

Prayer

Dear Lord, transform me into the kind of servant who will experience
Your love as fully as Jesus did. Amen.

Core Thought

> Compassion in ministry is sharing
> a common passion with Jesus.

Compassion is an interesting word. It is used mostly to convey the idea
of one person feeling pity for another and desiring that their suffering
be relieved, and there is much truth in that notion. But we mean this
and something more profound as well. Having compassion means to
share someone else's passion. To have *com-passion* means to have in
*com*mon *passion*. The meaning of passion is more difficult to grasp, but
it is worth the effort.

There are two ideas at work in the word *passion*. The first is the
idea that something is happening to us. That is what the prefix *pas*
means—an action is happening to us, we are *pas*sive. Something
outside of ourselves causes something inside ourselves to act. We are all
familiar with the idea of something arousing the passion within us. The
second idea at work involves suffering. One cannot escape the associa-
tion of the word passion with the notion of enduring suffering. We find
it not only in a Christian context (e.g., Christ's suffering on the cross

is referred to as Christ's Passion). We find it, interestingly enough, in secular contexts. Here's where it gets interesting.

The idea of passion in secular contexts has, from as far back in literature as we can recall, contained the idea of suffering, but most interestingly the suffering experienced was the result of the sufferer's love for someone. If we combine these ideas about having in common, of something outside of ourselves arousing something inside to act, and suffering as a consequence of having love for someone, we will begin to form the more profound understanding of what it means for us to have Jesus' compassion in ministry (Matthew 9:35-38).

To have compassion in ministry means that we share a common passion with Jesus. We are being motivated to serve by the same power that moved Jesus to serve, the power of the Spirit of God. The Holy Spirit stirs up within us our passion to love others, which we have from being made in God's image. His stirring causes the passion to love others to move us to act in obedience to Jesus' commands. Our obedience shows that we love Jesus; we love by serving our brothers and sisters in Christ and our neighbors. As our passion to love continues to be stirred by the Holy Spirit and as our obedience to Jesus' commands strengthens our perseverance, there grows within us the willingness to endure the suffering that conflict will bring as we minister to others in Jesus' name.

To minister as Jesus ministered is to share His source of motivation, His passion to love others, His expressions of love by serving others, and His willingness to suffer while serving those whom He loves. It is serving others.

Today's Exercises
Core Scripture: 2 Corinthians 7:1-13
Read aloud 2 Corinthians 7:1-13.
Recite this week's memory verse aloud five times.

> "My food," said Jesus, "is to do the will of him who sent me and to finish his work." (John 4:34)

Meditate on today's passage.

Request to Be in His Presence

"Dear Lord, bring me into the context of Your world."

1. ***Read it***—Remember: We read now only what is there, to hear once again, only what was spoken then. Read 1 Peter 4:1-2 at least twice, out loud.
2. ***Think it***—select a portion, a phrase within the reading, and mull it over in your mind, thinking about the context and setting, reimagining the event, putting yourself into the situation. As you meditate, use all five senses to re-create the context and the setting by building the images that are supplied within the passages.
3. ***Pray it***—ask God to give you understanding into how the truths He has spoken in these Scriptures apply to you now. Ask, "What is it about me that I need to deal with? What is it about me that must change?"

   Respond to God by accepting and admitting whatever responsibility is implied by what He has shown. Write what it is that God has shown you, and what you must admit responsibility for having done (or not done).
4. ***Live it***—ask God to reveal to you what He wants you to do about what you have admitted.

State what God has revealed that you must admit responsibility for doing.

State what particular action(s) you will take today to accomplish what God has revealed for you to do.

Journal

Record ideas, impressions, feelings, questions, and any insights you may have had during today's time.

Prayer

Pray for each member of your community.

Compassion in Ministry

DAY TWO

Prayer

Dear Lord, use me today to be your presence in this small corner of the world where I live, work, play, and worship. Help me not to overlook people and their needs. Give me an opportunity today to love someone in a way that will cause them to be conscious of Your presence. Amen.

Core Thought

> Compassion in ministry is sharing
> a common place with Jesus.

Another of Jesus' passions that we will share is the desire to be with the people we serve. To minister as Jesus ministered means that we will live with those whom we serve. It means that we understand our place of ministry to be wherever we can be Jesus to other people. We believe that the Lord has called us to serve those with whom we live, work, play, and worship. When we do so, the result will be that many will believe.

When Jesus began His public ministry He had no home for Himself. "Foxes have holes and birds of the air have nests, but the Son of Man has no place to lay his head" (Matthew 8:20). Instead, He made His home among those whom He served.

So when the Samaritans came to him, they urged him to stay with them, and he stayed two days. And because of his words many more became believers. They said to the woman, "We no longer believe just because of what you said; now we have heard for ourselves, and we know that this man really is the Savior of the world." (John 4:40-42)

It should be noted that unlike most Christians, Jesus dedicated His years of ministry in the company of unbelievers and not in the exclusive company of believers.

Jesus' place of ministry was with anyone the Father led Him to serve. His place of service was determined by the people He served. That is why we find Him serving in the synagogue (Luke 4:16), at dinner with a disciple's friends (Luke 5:27-29), at a party (John 2:1-11), in private conversations with leaders (John 3:1-21), and in public places with outcasts (John 4:5-26).

To minister as Jesus ministered we must share His passion to be with the people whom God calls us to serve.

Today's Exercises
Core Scripture: 2 Corinthians 7:1-13
Read aloud 2 Corinthians 7:1-13.
Recite this week's memory verse aloud five times.

"My food," said Jesus, "is to do the will of him who sent me and to finish his work." (John 4:34)

Meditate on today's passage.

Request to Be in His Presence
"Dear Lord, bring me into the context of Your world."

1. *Read it*—Remember: We read now only what is there, to hear once again, only what was spoken then. Read 1 Peter 4:3-6 at least twice, out loud.
2. *Think it*—select a portion, a phrase within the reading, and mull it over in your mind, thinking about the context and setting, reimagining the event, putting yourself into the situation. As you

meditate, use all five senses to re-create the context and the setting by building the images that are supplied within the passages.

3. ***Pray it***—ask God to give you understanding into how the truths He has spoken in these Scriptures apply to you now. Ask, "What is it about me that I need to deal with? What is it about me that must change?"

   Respond to God by accepting and admitting whatever responsibility is implied by what He has shown. Write what it is that God has shown you, and what you must admit responsibility for having done (or not done).

4. ***Live it***—ask God to reveal to you what He wants you to do about what you have admitted.

State what God has revealed that you must admit responsibility for doing.

State what particular action(s) you will take today to accomplish what God has revealed for you to do.

Journal

Record ideas, impressions, feelings, questions, and any insights you may have had during today's time.

Prayer

Pray for each member of your community.

Compassion in Ministry

DAY THREE

Prayer

Dear Father, continue to chip away at the lie that is wedged so tightly in my mind that nothing good comes from suffering. Lord, (I'm almost too afraid to ask) please do whatever it takes to make me reject this lie and embrace my place of suffering for Your name and serving others in Your name. Amen.

Core Thought

> Compassion in ministry is sharing a common pain with Jesus.

To say that Jesus the Son of God identified with mankind is too sterile to describe the extent to which He became as we are. Our theology is too simple and our words too weak to give us more than a cursory understanding of what the Son of God did for us when He became a man. But however cursory our understanding may be, the picture that Scripture presents is clear. In it we see from the beginning that the ministry Jesus chose would involve personal suffering. He would have to endure pain to accomplish what the Father had called Him to do.

Not only did Jesus suffer the inconceivably torturous pain of being crucified, He also suffered the pains, great and small, that are common to all of us. His perfect compassion for those who were suffering was the constant source of His own suffering. He suffered because those whom He loved suffered. After the death of His friend Lazarus, Jesus suffered the heartfelt pain of Mary's disappointment and blame: "Lord, if you had been here, my brother would not have died" (John 11:32). Knowing the full extent of the suffering that death causes and feeling with Mary and her friends the bleakness and wrongness that death causes their souls to experience caused Jesus deep pain in His soul. "When Jesus saw her weeping, and the Jews who had come along with her also weeping, he was deeply moved in spirit and troubled" (John 11:33). Because He loves them, He felt their pain and it drove Him to tears: "Jesus wept. Then the Jews said, "See how he loved him!" (John 11:35-36).

Jesus' love for those He served caused Him to share in their suffering. And out of that common pain arose a passion to take whatever action is necessary to put an end to all their suffering:

> Jesus, once more deeply moved, came to the tomb. It was a cave with a stone laid across the entrance. "Take away the stone," he said. . . . Jesus called in a loud voice, "Lazarus, come out!" The dead man came out. . . . Therefore many of the Jews who had come to visit Mary, and had seen what Jesus did, put their faith in him. (John 11:38-45)

To minister as Jesus ministered, we will share the common pain that He was called to endure: "For it has been granted to you on behalf of Christ not only to believe on him, but also to suffer for him" (Philippians 1:29). It is by loving one another and our neighbors that we will be known as His disciples. And it is because of the suffering we endure as we serve others in Jesus' name that we will be transformed into the incomparably glorious likeness of Jesus: "The Spirit himself testifies with our spirit that we are God's children. Now if we are children, then we are heirs—heirs of God and co-heirs with Christ, if indeed we share in his sufferings in order that we may also share in his glory. I consider that our present sufferings are not worth comparing with the glory that will be revealed in us" (Romans 8:16-18).

Today's Exercises

Core Scripture: 2 Corinthians 7:1-13

Read aloud 2 Corinthians 7:1-13.

Recite this week's memory verse aloud five times.

> "My food," said Jesus, "is to do the will of him who sent me and to finish his work." (John 4:34)

Meditate on today's passage.

Request to Be in His Presence

"Dear Lord, bring me into the context of Your world."

1. *Read it*—Remember: We read now only what is there, to hear once again, only what was spoken then. Read 1 Peter 4:7-11 at least twice, out loud.

2. *Think it*—select a portion, a phrase within the reading, and mull it over in your mind, thinking about the context and setting, reimagining the event, putting yourself into the situation. As you meditate, use all five senses to re-create the context and the setting by building the images that are supplied within the passages.

3. *Pray it*—ask God to give you understanding into how the truths He has spoken in these Scriptures apply to you now. Ask, "What is it about me that I need to deal with? What is it about me that must change?"

   Respond to God by accepting and admitting whatever responsibility is implied by what He has shown. Write what it is that God has shown you, and what you must admit responsibility for having done (or not done).

4. *Live it*—ask God to reveal to you what He wants you to do about what you have admitted.

State what God has revealed that you must admit responsibility for doing.

State what particular action(s) you will take today to accomplish what God has revealed for you to do.

Journal

Record ideas, impressions, feelings, questions, and any insights you may have had during today's time.

Prayer

Pray for each member of your community.

Compassion in Ministry

DAY FOUR

Prayer

Father, I know that some of my tastes and the things that I prefer are not appropriate for anyone who desires to please You. Please use the various things that I will encounter in my workaday life to transform my tastes. Change my desires into preferences that when satisfied will bring You and me great pleasure. Amen.

Core Thought

> Compassion in ministry is sharing
> a common pleasure with Jesus.

Sharing a common pleasure with Jesus simply means that we develop a taste for enjoying the things that delighted Jesus. So a good thing to ask right off the bat is, "What are the things that gave Jesus pleasure?" and, "What did He enjoy, and what delighted Him?"

While there doesn't seem to be a place in the Bible where you can find anything such as a listing of "The Top 10 Things Jesus Enjoyed," there are plenty of places where we are told what the Lord finds delightful.

One thing that is instructive to notice is that we as the authors will make no distinction between what God the Father delighted in and what Jesus the Son found delightful. We do so intentionally because Jesus makes no distinction between what He desires and in what the Father takes delight. Jesus acquired His Father's tastes and learned to be delighted in the same things that the Father enjoyed. It is the same for anyone who partners with Jesus to do the Father's business.

We are told that if you really understand the Lord's heart, you will know the three things that delight Him:

> "But let him who boasts boast about this: that he understands and knows me, that I am the LORD, who exercises kindness, justice and righteousness on earth, for in these I delight," declares the LORD. (Jeremiah 9:24)

The Lord delights in exercising kindness, justice, and righteousness. The Hebrew word picture for *exercise* depicts someone pushing up a mound of earth; it is the idea of heaping up something into a hill. In this case, the Lord delights in heaping His kindness, justice, and righteousness on common people (those who are low) until He has lifted them up above the high and mighty people of the earth. It is God's way of saying that He intends to change the world by pouring out His kindness, justice, and righteousness on the poor, lowly, and exploited. He will change the landscape not by the cleverness and skill of the powerful, but by His love working through the humble. He delights in lifting up the humble and casting down those who exalt themselves.

To minister as Jesus ministered is to share in His pleasure of serving anyone regardless of their station in life. We will enjoy heaping kindness upon them and demonstrating our love for them by our generosity, honesty, and impartiality.

Today's Exercises
Core Scripture: 2 Corinthians 7:1-13
Read aloud 2 Corinthians 7:1-13.
Recite this week's memory verse aloud five times.

> "My food," said Jesus, "is to do the will of him who sent me and to finish his work." (John 4:34)

Meditate on today's passage.

Request to Be in His Presence

"Dear Lord, bring me into the context of Your world."

1. ***Read it***—Remember: We read now only what is there, to hear once again, only what was spoken then. Read 1 Peter 4:12-15 at least twice, out loud.

2. ***Think it***—select a portion, a phrase within the reading, and mull it over in your mind, thinking about the context and setting, reimagining the event, putting yourself into the situation. As you meditate, use all five senses to re-create the context and the setting by building the images that are supplied within the passages.

3. ***Pray it***—ask God to give you understanding into how the truths He has spoken in these Scriptures apply to you now. Ask, "What is it about me that I need to deal with? What is it about me that must change?"

   Respond to God by accepting and admitting whatever responsibility is implied by what He has shown. Write what it is that God has shown you, and what you must admit responsibility for having done (or not done).

4. ***Live it***—ask God to reveal to you what He wants you to do about what you have admitted.

State what God has revealed that you must admit responsibility for doing.

State what particular action(s) you will take today to accomplish what God has revealed for you to do.

Journal

Record ideas, impressions, feelings, questions, and any insights you may have had during today's time.

Prayer

Pray for each member of your community.

Compassion in Ministry

DAY FIVE

Prayer

Dear Lord, grow in me a wonderful understanding of what partnership with You is all about. I know that the blessings must be fantastic and that the work must be the ultimate in satisfaction. Teach me, Lord. Amen.

Core Thought

> Compassion in ministry is sharing
> a common partnership with Jesus.

To minister in Jesus' name means that we share the passion Jesus has for doing the work of our Father's business. We will partner with Jesus to do the ministry that the Father entrusted to Jesus, reconciling the people of this world back to the heavenly Father who loves them.

To be partners in the family business means that we must take seriously our call to be the servant of anyone whom the Lord delivers into our sphere of influence (where we live, work, play, and worship). We will be highly committed to truth and faithful in continuing to obey His calling. Our conduct will show that we understand what our mission is and that we are wholeheartedly dedicated to accomplishing it with humility and graciousness.

Partnership with Jesus means that we will live within a community of believers to acquire the ability to serve others. By celebrating with our community we will maintain our availability to minister to others.

We know that partnership is not just a call to serve. It is also a call to suffer as Jesus suffered. Like Jesus, we choose to obey and remain faithful to our call and endure whatever suffering the conflicts will bring rather than compromise. We will stand firm against the weight of culture, tradition, and the allure of transient peace, holding fast to the truth of God's Word, serving in His power, and waiting for our blessed Hope, the everlasting Prince of Peace. Until then, we will be found ministering in Jesus' name to the people Jesus loves, enjoying their company, sharing in their tears, and being delighted by the opportunity to minister as Jesus ministered.

Today's Exercises

Core Scripture: 2 Corinthians 7:1-13

Read aloud 2 Corinthians 7:1-13.

Recite this week's memory verse aloud five times.

> "My food," said Jesus, "is to do the will of him who sent me and to finish his work." (John 4:34)

Meditate on today's passage.

Request to Be in His Presence

"Dear Lord, bring me into the context of Your world."

1. *Read it*—Remember: We read now only what is there, to hear once again, only what was spoken then. Read 1 Peter 4:16-19 at least twice, out loud.

2. *Think it*—select a portion, a phrase within the reading, and mull it over in your mind, thinking about the context and setting, reimagining the event, putting yourself into the situation. As you meditate, use all five senses to re-create the context and the setting by building the images that are supplied within the passages.

3. *Pray it*—ask God to give you understanding into how the truths He has spoken in these Scriptures apply to you now. Ask, "What is it about me that I need to deal with? What is it about me that must change?"

Respond to God by accepting and admitting whatever responsibility is implied by what He has shown. Write what it is that God has shown you, and what you must admit responsibility for having done (or not done).

4. *Live it*—ask God to reveal to you what He wants you to do about what you have admitted.

State what God has revealed that you must admit responsibility for doing.

State what particular action(s) you will take today to accomplish what God has revealed for you to do.

Journal

Record ideas, impressions, feelings, questions, and any insights you may have had during today's time.

Prayer

Pray for each member of your community.

Compassion in Ministry

DAY SIX

Community Meeting

In preparation for this week's meeting, you will have read and reflected upon each of the week's five Core Thoughts, recorded your thoughts and observations, and are ready to recite this week's memory verse to the group.

ABOUT THE AUTHORS

BILL HULL's mission is to call the church to return to its disciple-making roots. He is a writer and discipleship evangelist calling the church to *choose the life*, a journey that Jesus called every disciple to pursue. This journey leads to a life of spiritual transformation and service. A veteran pastor, Bill has written ten books on this subject. In 1990 he founded T-NET International, a ministry devoted to transforming churches into disciple-making churches.

The core of Bill's writing is *Jesus Christ, Disciplemaker*; *The Disciple-Making Pastor*; and *The Disciple-Making Church*. He now spends his time helping leaders experience personal transformation so they can help transform their churches.

Bill and his wife, Jane, enjoy their not-so-quiet life, helping to raise their "highly energetic" grandchildren, in the beautiful Southern California sunshine.

PAUL MASCARELLA has served in local church ministry for more than twenty-five years as an associate pastor, minister of music, and worship director while holding an executive management position at a daily newspaper in Los Angeles, California. He is associate director of *Choose the Life Ministries*, where the abundance of his time and energy go to assisting churches as they embark on The *Choose the Life Journey*, and proceed forward with the EXPERIENCE THE LIFE series. He also serves on the board of directors for Bill Hull Ministries. He holds the Bachelor of Philosophy and Master of Theological Studies degrees.

Paul and his wife, Denise, reside in Southern California.

ALSO BY
BILL HULL

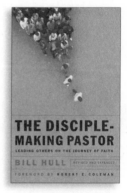

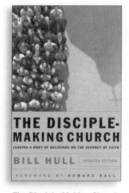

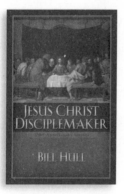

The Disciple-Making Pastor,
rev. & exp. ed.

The Disciple-Making Church,
updated ed.

Jesus Christ, Disciplemaker,
20th ann. ed.

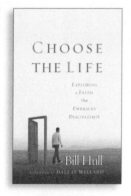

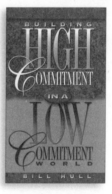

Choose the Life

Building High Commitment
in a Low-Commitment World

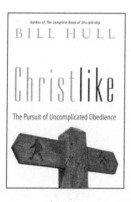